Photography & Culture

Volume 2—Issue 2—July 2009

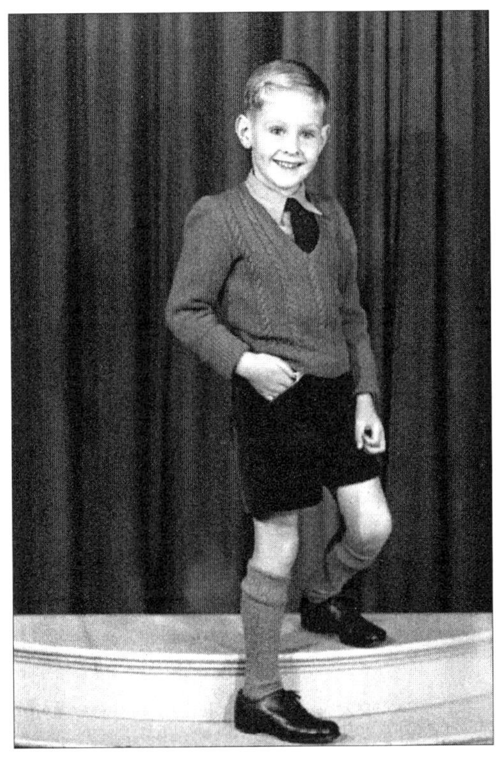

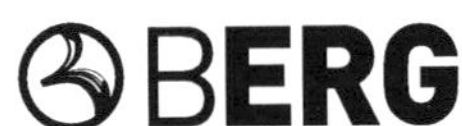

Editors

Kathy Kubicki
Alison Nordström
Val Williams

Aims and Scope

Photography & Culture is a new refereed journal that will be international in its scope and inter-disciplinary in its contributions. It aims to interrogate the contextual and historic breadth of photographic practice from a range of informed perspectives and to encourage new insights into the media through original and incisive writing.

Photography & Culture publishes research papers, discursive critiques and reviews. It appears at a key moment as photography evolves; once again, to embrace a technological change that is shifting both contemporary usage and historic understanding.

Photography & Culture will quickly establish itself as a leading platform for critical thinking on photography and as essential reading the world over for academics, curators and practitioners with a central and indeed tangential interest in the media.

Submissions

To submit an article for consideration please contact Monica Takvam at photographyandculture@bergpublishers.com

Subscription Information
Three issues per volume (only two issues in 2008). One volume per annum. 2009: volume 2

Online
www.bergpublishers.com

By Mail
Berg Publishers
C/o Customer Services
Turpin Distribution
Pegasus Drive
Stratton Business Park
Biggleswade
Bedfordshire SG18 8TQ
UK

By Fax
+44 (0)1767 601640

By Telephone
+44 (0)1767 604951

Subscription Rates
Institutional
Print and Online: 1 year: £155/US$302; 2 year: £248/US$484
Online only: 1 year: £132/US$257; 2 year £211/US$411 (VAT charged as applicable)

Individual
Print: 1 year: £35/US$65; 2 year: £55/US$105

Full color images available online
Access your electronic subscription through **www.ingentaconnect.com**

Reprints for Mailing
Copies of individual articles may be obtained from the publishers at the appropriate fees. For information, write to

Berg Publishers
1st Floor, Angel Court
81 St Clements Street
Oxford OX4 1AW
UK

Inquiries
Editorial:
Julia Hall, email: jhall@bergpublishers.com

Production:
Ken Bruce, email: kbruce@bergpublishers.com

Advertising:
Corina Kapinos, email: ckapinos@bergpublishers.com

Berg Publishers is a member of CrossRef

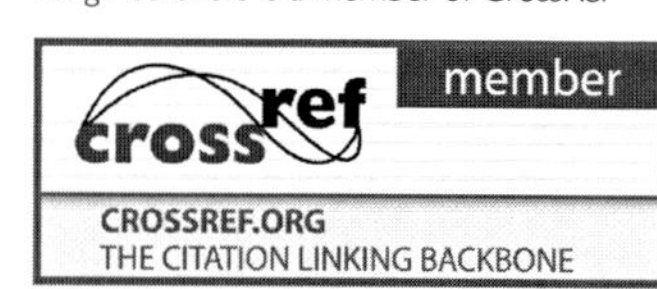

Photography & Culture

Volume 2—Issue 2—July 2009

Contents

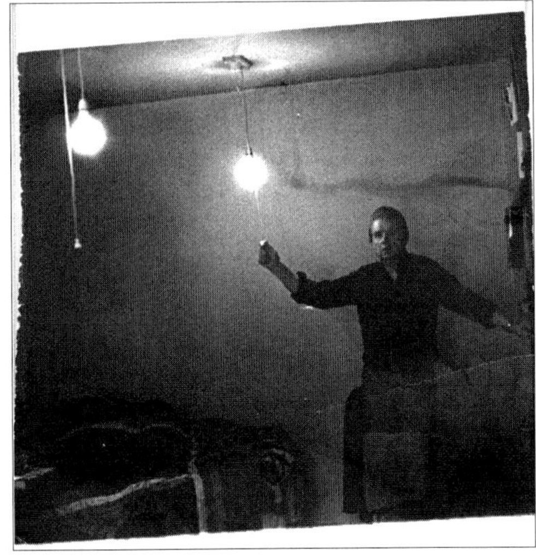

**Photography
& Culture**

Volume 2—Issue 2
July 2009
pp. 117–118
DOI:
10.2752/175145109X12456654102641

From the Editors

This issue of *Photography & Culture* focuses on the position of the archive in reflections upon contemporary photography and looks at its relationship with performativity, with history and psychology, with the ways in which we resource it for information about culture and society.

In her powerful essay "Performing the Relational Archive," Merav Yerushalmy constructs a discussion of the discourse of photographic theory, highlighting aspects of its recent history as well as contemporary practices to address today's socially engaged art, and exploring the roles photography plays within it. Yerushalmy's terrain is wide ranging and fascinating, exploring how "socially engaged" art has become a major strand in contemporary production, and the ways in which it has used and intervened in a wide variety and range of archives. Citing artists such as Mark Dion, Tacita Dean and Renee Green, Yerushalmy embarks on an exacting journey through the work of artists and curators who used the archive to: "explore the critical potency of what has been left to them."

Psychologists Michael Stones and Marlee Bargate, in their paper "Emotive Factors that Make Photographs Memorable" ask a fundamental question: "How do ordinary people respond to photographs?" Using the psychologist's model of "incidental memory" they describe the reactions of two groups of participants to a series of photographs from the archive International Affective Picture System. The results of this experiment are described in detail in the paper that Stones and Barlee have written. For those of us who curate, make and reflect upon photography's place in the world, the results are fascinating.

Following the theme of archive, Jane Tynan explores the ways in which the male military body was represented in press photographs from the Second World War, alerting us to the development of news management as photography began its meteoric rise as a major transmitter of event. In her "Research in Progress" essay, Francesca Kubicki discusses the ways in which photography was used to document facial injuries (and subsequent surgery) in the First World War, with particular reference to the albums compiled by reconstructive surgeon Harold Gilles. Both Tynan and Kubicki have researched archives of conflict, asking very different questions about how we decipher the past through the medium of photography.

For the "Archive" section, Kathy Kubicki has explored the Francis Bacon holdings at the Tate Archive—few artists have fascinated the outside world more than Bacon, and Kubicki's trawl of these "domestic" photographs produces—as domestic photographs always do—clues to reconstruct the space between public and private.

Each issue of a journal is in itself an archive. This one looks at the partialness of archive, the fascination with fragmentation, the bringing of the past into the present, the participation of artists, curators and all of us in the archive's journey from past to present.

The Editors
Photography & Culture

**Photography
& Culture**

Volume 2—Issue 2
July 2009
pp. 119–134
DOI:
10.2752/175145109X12456654102687

Emotive Factors that Make Photographs Memorable

Michael J. Stones and Marlee Bygate

Michael Stones is Professor of Psychology at Lakehead
University. He is the author of two books for the general
market, a popular textbook, two books on research and over
150 book chapters and research articles. Photography is both
a passion and a focus of research for him. Marlee Bygate is a
graduate of Lakehead University. The findings described here
were part of her thesis research.

Abstract
Fleeting exposure to photographic images in newspapers,
magazines, advertisements and elsewhere is part of
everyday life. Some of these images stick in our memory
while we quickly forget others. This article reviews
previous research, provides a theoretical model and
presents new findings to elucidate emotive influences that
make photographs memorable. Earlier research identified
pleasantness and arousal as the main emotions elicited
by photographs. The new study used an experimental
design that manipulated level of emotion (anxiety) before
viewing photographs. Specifically, participants either
received or did not receive emotive priming before
viewing a set of fifty-seven photographs, each exposed
for six seconds. They rated each photograph on emotive
measures immediately after exposure and recalled as
many photographs as possible after viewing the full set.
The findings show that emotion induced by priming
affected both emotive appraisal and which photographs
viewers recalled. Anxious viewers were more likely to
appraise photographs as unpleasant, with higher recall of
photographs appraised as unpleasant. All viewers recalled
more photographs appraised as arousing rather than
quiescent. The findings are consistent with a model of
emotion and memory that has relevance to understanding

the reception of photographs throughout the social sciences and humanities.

Keywords: arousal, emotion, memory, photographs, photography, pleasantness, recall, unpleasantness

Introduction

This article reviews previous literature and reports new research findings on emotive factors that make photographs memorable. It begins by locating photography with personal and cultural contexts. This is followed by an outline of the disciplinary perspective that informs the research and then by discussion of theory and previous research on memory for photographs, and presentation of an integrative model. The subsequent sections explain the rationale for new research, describe its methodology, report findings and discuss their significance and implications.

Personal and Cultural Contexts of Photography

How do ordinary people respond to photographs? Not photographs on a gallery wall that enthusiasts and connoisseurs make a point of going to see but less renowned pictures of objects, people, or events that might appear in a newspaper, a magazine, or as part of an advertisement. They are photographs that pass by us during the ongoing stream of daily life with no attempt made to fix them in memory. If they ever come to mind again, psychologists call it incidental memory. Incidental memory includes the scores or even hundreds of photographs each of us sees during the course of a day.

Which (if any) of that myriad of photographs do we remember? Are they more likely to be concrete than abstract depictions, emotive rather than neutral scenes, pleasant rather than disturbing images? Does existing state of mind when viewing the pictures affect which ones we recall? The answers are of interest to commerce, the media, advertisers and anyone interested in social influence, to cite but some examples. They are also of interest to academics trying to understand memory processes within individuals and the transmission of memories into culture.

Memory is not just an individual experience but also a collective phenomenon. If cultural understanding relates to meaning and symbols, then memory has relevance to continuity and change within a culture (Nora 2002). Likewise, photography has significance for cultural transition. Taking photographs can be part of a ritual or rite of passage (as in wedding or school photography). News photography establishes the importance of the people or event depicted. Photographs can serve as records, memorials, aids to memory and tools used in research (Harper 2002); they can override or substitute for memories (Keenan 1998; Sturken 1999). They can be works of art or expropriated into works of art (Langford 2008). Then again, photographers might be unwelcome, intruders (paparazzi, for instance)—their practice thought an exploitation (Sontag 1977).

The transmission of memory into culture—whether personal or photographic—is fluid and open to change. Personal memories change when recounted to others. The latter place their own interpretations on recounted memories, with the narrator also likely to recollect differently next time around. An example is eyewitness testimony, research on which shows that two people viewing the same event may remember it differently, with changes in those memories over time. Photographs, as surrogate memory traces, also transcend personal experience. Viewers differ in their appraisal and memory of the same photograph. A viewer may appraise and interpret it differently on repeated exposure. Like memory traces embedded in the soft tissue of the brain, repeated exposure to a photograph brings about emotive attenuation known to psychologists as *extinction*. Just as memories of past joy or grief fade towards neutrality with time, a photograph loses its capacity to excite or shock with repeated viewing. It is for this reason that older memories and surrogate photographic traces move us less than do their newer equivalents.

Psychological research

Psychology is the science of behavior. Behavior is an observable outcome of complex and interrelated influences that include personality traits and dispositions, emotions and feelings, previous life experience, and physical and social situations that provide an immediate context for that behavior. Research psychologists try to understand the influences on behavior through reductive procedures that include measurement, simplification and control.

Measurement is a key element. Researchers attempt to make implicit concepts explicit by means of measurement. Measurement of memory, for example, might reduce to whether a person is able or unable to recall an earlier occurrence, or to enumeration of details about that event. Even emotions and feelings are amenable to measurement based on emotive statements, emotive signals or facial expression. Along with questions about the reliability and validity of measurement, which preoccupy psychologists, interpretation of research findings usually involves statistical analysis of the distributions and interrelationships of measures.

The purpose of simplification and control is to focus the research on just those behaviors and influences that the researcher considers to be important. The pre-eminent approach to methodology is through experimental design, which manipulates important influences on behavior and attempts to control for unwanted influences. For example, the new research reported in this article assigned participants to groups that received different levels of emotive priming prior to viewing photographs. In order to control for unwanted influences, the assignment of participants to groups was random. Consequently, differences between these groups on subsequent measures of emotive appraisal and memory should reflect only emotive manipulation rather than systematic differences between participants assigned to one or other group.

What we know about emotive appraisal and memory of photographs

Principles that direct scientific knowledge about the emotive appraisal and memory of photographs derive from two main theories. Modern research on emotive appraisal dates from seminal work by Osgood, Suci and Tannenbaum (1967). Their research indentified dimensions of meaning shared by humans regardless of cultural background, as evidenced by studies in more than twenty cultures around the world (Heise 2001; Osgood, May and Miron 1975).

Applied to emotive appraisal, the two main dimensions are the pleasant-unpleasant (hedonic) and the aroused-quiescent continuums. Measurement scales for these continuums include five-point adjectival ratings and self-assessment manikins. The latter include five manikins per scale, each of which depicts a different level on the respective continuum.

Influences on emotive appraisal include immediate sources of stimulation and ongoing motivational states that precede that stimulation. Modern theories suggest that both contribute to appetitive or defensive inclinations (tendencies to approach versus running away or fighting) that humans share with other species (Bradley, Codispoti, Sabatinelli and Lang 2001).

Theories about stages of memory build on those proposed in the nineteenth century by William James (Atkinson and Shiffrin 1968; James 1890). The process begins with the sensory information that enters a short-term store known as *working memory* (Baddeley 2000). We are conscious of content within this store, with the work done there a determinant of whether we forget that content or enable its entry into long-term memory (Craik and Lockhart 1972). A term used to describe this work is encoding. *Encoding* relates to the content's meaning and the linkages formed with memories already present in long-term memory. The final stage is retrieval, which can take two forms. One form is recall that applies to memory for something not present at the time of retrieval. The other is recognition,

when something now present might be a recurrence of something present an earlier time.

We actually know quite a lot about emotive appraisal and memory of photographs. First, we process sensory information to identify what the content depicts (for example, a dog, person, building or landscape). It takes about 0.1 seconds to identify photographic content in short-term memory, with a further 0.3 seconds needed for that memory to become robust (Potter 1976).

Second, photographs that elicit emotion do so very quickly. Junghofer, Bradley, Elbert and Lang (2001) exposed viewers to 700 pictures at rates of three or five per second, finding discrimination of emotive from neutral content in the brain's visual system. A later study by Bradley, Hamby, Löw and Lang (2007) confirmed that this discrimination occurred immediately after the identification phase. Consequently, we know that the brain registers identity and emotion within the first second after exposure to a photograph.

Third, the next few seconds of processing flesh out the meaning of a photograph in working memory. Axelsson (2007) found that the main dimensions used to evaluate the meaning of 564 photographs included three for content and two for emotive appraisal. The former are familiarity, presence or absence of color, and dynamics (level of activity); the latter are dimensions of pleasantness and arousal (intensity of emotion) that we mentioned in the last section.

Fourth, Axelsson (2007) showed correlations between ratings of content and emotive appraisal. Although it is a truism that correlation does not prove causation, research already referred to indicates that identification of content is a precursor to (and therefore is a causal influence on) emotive appraisal. What Axelsson (2007) found was that viewers rated photographs with familiar content as more pleasant than unpleasant and pictures with active content as more arousing than quiescent. Although the expectedness of the latter negates any need for elaboration, reasons for an association of familiarity with pleasantness may be less clear. However, an abundance of evidence anticipates feelings of comfort with photographs of known meaning but relative discomfort with those of indeterminate meaning (Rosenblatt, Greenberg, Solomon, Pyszczynski and Lyon 1989). An example is that the provision of titles to assist identification causes a shift in ratings of pictures, photographs, and paintings toward the pleasant pole of the pleasant-unpleasant continuum (Landau, Greenberg, Solomon, Pyszczynzki and Martens 2006; Mills 2001; Russell 2003). In other words, familiarity or content that contributes to meaningfulness (such as titles) makes an appraisal of pleasantness more likely. On the other hand, content dimensions without bearing on meaning do not correlate with emotive appraisal. These dimensions include the size of an image and the presence or absence of color (Sánchez-Navarro, Martínez-Selva, Román and Ginesa 2006).

Fifth, memory for photographs varies with the emotion elicited. Bradley, Greenwald, Petry and Lang (1992) found higher recall and recognition of photographs rated as arousing rather than quiescent. Christianson and Fällman (1990) found higher recognition of unpleasant pictures than pleasant or neutral pictures. Anderson, Wais and Gabrieli (2006) found that recognition of pictures presented early in a sequence was higher if subsequent pictures were emotionally arousing rather than bland. Differences in methodology and purpose across studies make these findings seem somewhat of a hodgepodge but they are consistent in that photographs eliciting emotion facilitate memory compared with emotionally neutral pictures.

Sixth, prior exposure to photographs can affect the reproduction of personal memories across a social matrix. Examples include findings from eyewitness testimony research. Deffenbacher, Bornstein and Penrod (2006) studied the effects of viewing mugshots between the crime scene and lineup phases of simulated criminal activity. There were more errors by witnesses shown mugshots before the lineups than those without such exposure. Such findings are consistent with theory and studies initiated by Bartlett (1932), which continues to inform cultural and social studies of the transmission of personal information (Johnston 2001).

A model of emotive appraisal and memory of photographs

Theory and research discussed in the preceding section suggest a general model in which motivational state affects emotive encoding in working memory, which in turn affects level of retrieval from long-term memory. Figure 1 illustrates the model, with motivational states classified into defensive or appetitive tendencies described by Bradley, Codispoti, Sabatinelli and Lang (2001). The presence of defensive motivation makes threatening content more salient in working memory, with effects on subsequent retrieval from long-term memory. Similarly, the presence of appetitive motivation makes

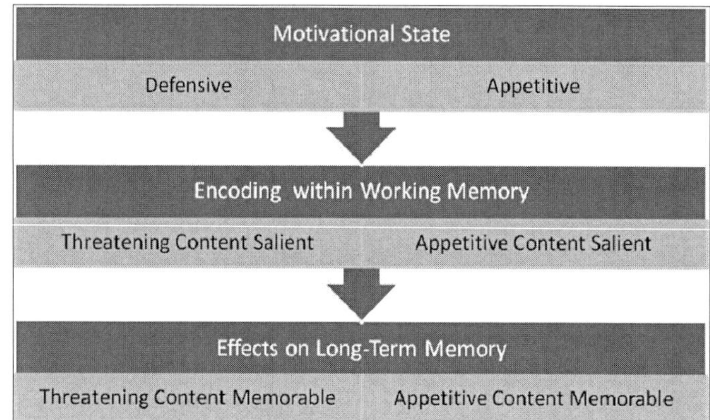

Fig 1 Model of the effects of motivational state on working memory and long-term memory.

compatible content more salient in working memory and retrievable from long-term memory. The following research tests aspects of the model.

Rationale for the Present Study

The purpose was to test an application of the model intended to clarify the hodgepodge of effects obtained from studies of emotive appraisal and subsequent memory of photographs, and to advance empirical knowledge beyond its current level. The methodology builds on seminal research by Bradley, Greenwald, Petry and Lang (1992); however, inclusion of a prior stage of emotive manipulation makes the present design a truly experimental study. The reasons for such inclusion are:

- Prior emotional state is known to affect the emotive appraisal of pictures.

- Emotive appraisal is known to affect which photographs are more memorable.

- However, no study to date has examined the effects of prior emotional state on emotive appraisal and memory. We think that complete inclusion is necessary to advance knowledge.

Figure 2 depicts the general model mentioned above adapted to the design used in the present research. Prior emotional state reflects the level of defensive motivation, manipulated in the design to correspond with the presence or absence of anxiety. Emotive appraisal reflects encoding within working memory as measured on pleasant-unpleasant and aroused-quiescent continuums. Measurement of recall represents the effects on long-term memory. A rationale for the causal expectations in Figure 2 follows.

First, the purpose of the emotive manipulation was to induce a state termed *existential anxiety* though the use of procedures shown to be effective in earlier research (Rosenblatt, Greenberg, Solomon, Pyszczynski and Lyon 1989; Rosenblatt, Greenberg, Solomon, Pyszczynski and

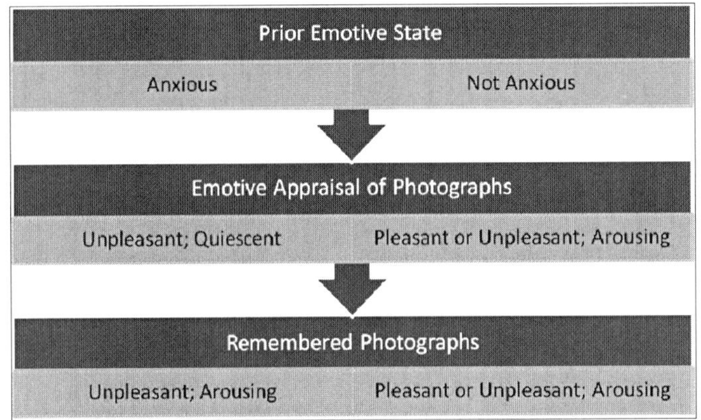

Fig 2 A model of predicted relationships between prior emotive state, emotive appraisal of photographs and memory of photographs.

Lyon 1989). Psychologists understand anxiety to be a form of unpleasant arousal and a defensive (rather than appetitive) motivational state (Corr 2008; Staal 2004).

Second, the anticipated effects of anxiety include shifts in the appraisal of pictures toward unpleasantness on the pleasant-unpleasant continuum (Landau, Greenberg, Solomon, Pyszczynzki and Martens 2006; Rawlings 2003) and quiescence on the arousing-quiescent continuum. The latter occurs because anxious people attribute their arousal an inner condition and encode external sources of visual arousal less effectively (Koster, Crombez, Veschuere and De Houwer 2006; Tuller and Pinto 2005; Valentine and Mesout 2009).

Third, the anticipated effects of emotive appraisal on memory are clear for the arousal-quiescence continuum. Previous findings are consistent that arousing photographs are more memorable than quiescent photographs. However, previous findings are inconsistent about the significance of the pleasant-unpleasant

continuum for memory (Bradley, Greenwald, Petry and Lang 1992; Christianson and Fällman 1990). Reasons for the latter probably relate to the methods of statistical analysis used by the researchers.

Fourth, the model anticipates differences in the recall of photographs appraised as pleasant or unpleasant depending on the presence or absence of anxiety, which is a defensive motivational state. In the absence of anxiety, appraisal of photographs as pleasant or unpleasant (as opposed to hedonically neutral) should augment their salience for encoding in working memory, with resulting effects of higher recall. This was the finding obtained by Christianson and Fällman (1990). However, the presence of defensive motivation directs attention toward sources of threat. Unpleasantness signifies threat so photographs appraised as unpleasant should be the most salient in working memory, with undue encoding resulting in disproportionately higher recall. Consequently, the model predicts interactive effects between level of anxiety and hedonic appraisal on memory for photographs.

Research Methods

The participants were forty university students randomly assigned to treatment and control groups and tested individually. Technical problems resulted in omission of analyzable data from one participant. Each completed an initial survey that differed between groups with respect to two open-ended questions. The purpose of the questions in the version completed by the treatment group was to induce anxiety about personal mortality. Participants responded to these questions by relating thoughts about what would physically happen to them when dying and what emotions those thoughts elicited (Greenberg, Solomon, Pyszczynski and Lyon 1989). The dummy questions posed to the control group had the same phrasing but with content that referred to their next meal rather than anything likely to induce anxiety.

Following a brief training period, participants viewed fifty-seven photographs from an archive extensively used in previous research (International Affective Picture System—Lang, Bradley and Cuthbert 1997). The photographs chosen were comparable in content to those used by Bradley, Greenwald, Petry and Lang (1992). The archivists prohibit the display of any photographs in public or academic media (to prevent contamination of subsequent research) so Table 1 contains only brief descriptions of the photographs. All were 1024 × 768 pixel color images suitable for computer presentation. Exposure to each photograph was for 6 seconds, after which participants rated it on previously

described five-point pleasant-unpleasant and aroused-quiescent scales with graphic self-assessment manikins (for example, the manikins at the extremes of the pleasantness scale were a smiling face and a scowling face). A considerable body of previous research attests to the reliable use of these measures, with extensive normative data (collected by the archivists) on ratings for the photographs used. Presentation and ratings of the photographs were by computer, with three random orders of presentation.

Table 1 Brief description of the photographs

Snake	Man in bed	Urban building
Spider	Romantic couple	City landscape
Horse	Couple in bed	Ski jumper
Rabbit	Mountains	Sailing
Coyote	River	Gymnast
Cow	Beach at sunset	Tennis player
Woman on beach	Gun pointed away	Pole vaulter
Angry woman	Gun pointed toward	War graves
Man and baby	Bomber aircraft	Barbed wire
Neutral man	Missile range	Starving child
Elderly man	Rolling pin	Airplane crash
Elderly woman	Hair dryer	Solemn boy
Mutilated face	Garbage bin	Electrical wires
Burn victim	Umbrella	Car exhaust
Mutilated body	Light bulb	Dirty puddle
Bloody finger	Turkey dinner	Animal carcass
Surgery	Cake	Soldier
Woman in water	Chocolate soda	Dead seals
Man on beach	Wine	African woman

Finally, participants recalled as many photographs as they could by providing written descriptions. In order to test the reliability of the recall measure, two judges independently assessed which photographs participants recalled. The research took about 45 minutes for each participant.

Results of the Study

Preliminary analyses examined the reliability of the recall measure, distributional properties on all the measures and sex differences. First, the two judges showed very high agreement about the number of photographs that participants recalled (a reliability coefficient of 0.95). Second, mean levels on the recall and emotive appraisal measures were near the midpoints on the respective scales, with 46 percent of photographs recalled, and mean scores of 2.9 and 2.7 on five-point pleasant-unpleasant and aroused-quiescent scales. Third, the groups contained comparable numbers of males and females, with no significant differences between the sexes on any of the measures. Consequently, the findings from the preliminary analyses provide evidence of reliability, an absence of skew in any distribution, and comparability of those distributions between males and females.

The main analyses used *Generalized Estimating Equations* in version 16 of the Statistical Package for the Social Sciences. These equations enable analysis of the full data set while taking account of the type and shape of the distributions of scores and relationships between repeated measures. For all the analyses, unconstrained relationships between the repeated measures provided best fit to the data.

The first analysis related the pleasant-unpleasant ratings to groups and photographs. Statistical significance is given in terms of probability levels so that $p < 0.05$ means one in 20, $p < 0.01$ means one in 100, and so on. Only levels of $p < 0.05$ or less

are considered significant. Significant findings, depicted in Figure 3, were that:

- Ratings differed across photographs ($p < 0.001$).

- The treatment group rated photographs as more unpleasant than did the control Group ($p < 0.01$).

The second analysis related the aroused-quiescent ratings to groups and photographs. Significant findings were that:

- Ratings differed across photographs ($p < 0.001$).

- The treatment group rated the photographs as less arousing than did the control group ($p < 0.03$) (see Figure 3).

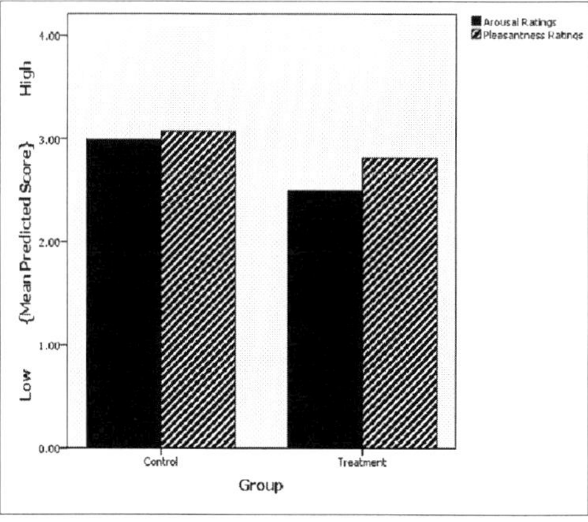

Fig 3 Mean predicted ratings by group. Lower ratings are toward the quiescent pole of the aroused-quiescent scale and the unpleasant pole of the pleasant-unpleasant scale.

The final analysis evaluated the recall of photographs. With recall a binary index for each photograph, the measurement model was binary logistic. The predictors were groups, the two emotive rating measures, all their two-way interactions and photographs. Significant findings were that:

- Level of recall differed across photographs ($p < 0.001$).

- Recall was higher for photographs rated as arousing rather than those rated as quiescent ($p < 0.01$).

- Recall varied according to interactive effects between groups and pleasantness-unpleasantness ratings ($p < 0.005$).

Figure 4 shows the latter finding. Although recall of neutral photographs was lowest in both groups, the treatment group recalled

more photographs rated as unpleasant rather than as pleasant, whereas the control group recalled comparable numbers of photographs rated as pleasant or unpleasant. The anxiety manipulation, therefore, affected the balance between pleasant and unpleasant photographs that participants recalled.

Discussion

The findings provide strong support for the causal linkages derived from the general model (Figure 1) and applied to the present research design (Figure 2). The following summary includes congruencies between these findings and trends reported in previous research:

- Induced anxiety shifts emotive ratings toward the quiescent pole of the aroused-quiescent continuum (Koster, Crombez, Veschuere and De Houwer 2006; Tuller and Pinto 2005).

- Induced anxiety shifts emotive ratings toward the unpleasant pole of the pleasant-unpleasant continuum (Landau, Greenberg, Solomon, Pyszczynzki and Martens 2006).

- Recall is higher for photographs rated as arousing rather than quiescent (Bradley, Greenwald, Petry and Lang 1992).

- Recall varies with the interaction between the presence or absence of induced anxiety and ratings on the pleasant-unpleasant continuum— photographs rated as unpleasant have the highest level of recall when preceded by anxiety induction;

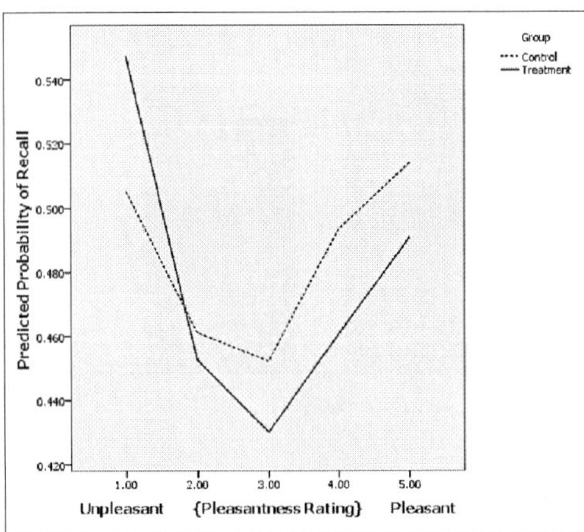

Fig 4 Predicted probability of recalling a photograph by pleasantness rating and group.

photographs rated as either pleasant or unpleasant have high levels of recall in the absence of induced anxiety; photographs rated as neutral have the lowest levels of recall (Christianson and Fällman 1990).

- Photographic content affects both emotive ratings and recall beyond any influence due to the presence or absence of induced anxiety.

The replications of previously established trends confirm that anxiety makes photographs seem unpleasant and quiescent and that arousing photographs are more memorable. Important new findings relate to the interactive effects of induced anxiety and hedonic appraisal on subsequent memory. This interaction not only clarifies inconsistencies in previous research but also advances empirical knowledge about memory for photographs.

The inconsistencies refer to findings that memory retrieval either fails to correlate with pleasantness-unpleasantness ratings (Bradley, Greenwald, Petry and Lang 1992) or is higher at either extreme than the midrange of this hedonic scale (Christianson and Fällman 1990). Findings for the control group replicate those from *both* studies, thereby showing that the disparity between them is ostensible rather than authentic. Figure 4 shows that the relationship between level of retrieval and hedonic ratings is **U**-shaped for the control group. With hedonic ratings analyzed as a continuous measure, the correlation with level of recall is near zero. However, with the hedonic ratings analyzed as categories (for example, as pleasant, neutral, and unpleasant) the

findings replicate those of Christianson and Fällman (1990). Consequently, the supposed inconsistency is resolvable by reference to different procedures for statistical analysis.

The advancement of knowledge derives from findings for the treatment group. Figure 4 shows that the relationship between level of recall and hedonic ratings approximates a **J**-shape, with higher recall of photographs rated as unpleasant. This finding is fully consistent with general model (Figure 1) applied to defensive motivation (Figure 2), wherein appraisal of unpleasantness signifies threat, the detection of threat augments salience within working memory, which results in higher capability in recall. The present research is the first to confirm the validity of this theoretical chain in an empirical study.

The general model has implications for photography that extend beyond those of the present study. The core proposition— that what makes photographs memorable includes the viewer's motivational state at the time of incidental exposure—refers to a broad dichotomy of motivations. The present study manipulated defensive motivation through induced anxiety. Anxiety alerts the viewer to any source of threat. Other forms of defensive motivation (such as fears or phobias) alert the viewer to specific threats. Therefore, the model predicts higher salience in working memory and higher recall of photographs depicting feared content when preceded by stimulation of specific fears. Implications of the model with respect to appetitive motivation include the following: a predicted shift in hedonic appraisal toward pleasantness, augmented salience in working memory and higher recall for photographs congruent with the appetitive desires. Such desires may be romantic or pragmatic, communal or solitary, but serve to fulfill a need rather than mitigate a threat. Consequently, it is easy to comprehend that the model is able to further our insights about a broad range of transitory motivations that help to make photographs memorable.

The scope of the model also includes enduring, rather than transitory, motivations that affect encoding. Enduring motivations provide an ever-present detection system for relevant threats or desires. Such motivations differ between people and across categories of people. They may help account for differences in the recall of photographs beyond the effects of transitory motivation studied in the present research.

Examples of the effects of enduring motivations on the encoding and retrieval of photographs include the following. Rawlings (2003) studied personality differences between people. He found that neuroticism and other traits influenced affective appraisals relevant to the encoding of pictures. Bradley, Codispoti, Sabatinelli and Lang (2001) reported on differences in emotive salience between men and women. They found that unpleasant pictures have higher emotive salience for women than men, whereas men show elevated appetitive responses only when viewing erotica. A supplementary analysis of the present data examined the content of photographs that were least memorable in men and women. Photographs of household utensils (rolling pin, hair dryer, and garbage can) were least memorable in men, with sports figures (gymnast, tennis player) least memorable for women. What all these findings illustrate is the dependence of encoding or memory on individual or group differences in the content of enduring motivations.

Other sources of defensive and appetitive motivation derive from personal histories, most of which remain undisclosed in quantitative research. An important aspect of personal history is relevance to self. The portrait of a boy in Figure 5 seems pleasant enough but rather bland and certainly not memorable. However, suppose you knew that boy as a child or grown-up. Suppose he were your son, brother, father or spouse. Even imagine that he were you. Then that photograph would be memorable indeed! The significance of self-relevance cannot be understated. For over fifty years, self-relevance continues to remain a cornerstone in psychological theories of self-concept (Rogers 1947), with the latter a key resource for the organization and regulation of emotion and cognition. Self-relevance is also within the technical and theoretical armories of anthropology and sociology, in which the use of photographs to help unlock or organize the recall of self-relevant memories goes by the term photo-elicitation (Harper 2002).

Although the focus of the present research was on motivation as a modifier of emotive evaluation and memory of photographs, the general model can provide a deeper understanding about the use of photographs to aid or prompt memory retrieval. Studies of photo-elicitation show that the presentation of pictures relevant to personal history can help to release a torrent of memories (Harper 2002). These photographs accentuate the self-concept as a motivational state, with memories that are congruent with threats and desires salient to the self-concept made more accessible.

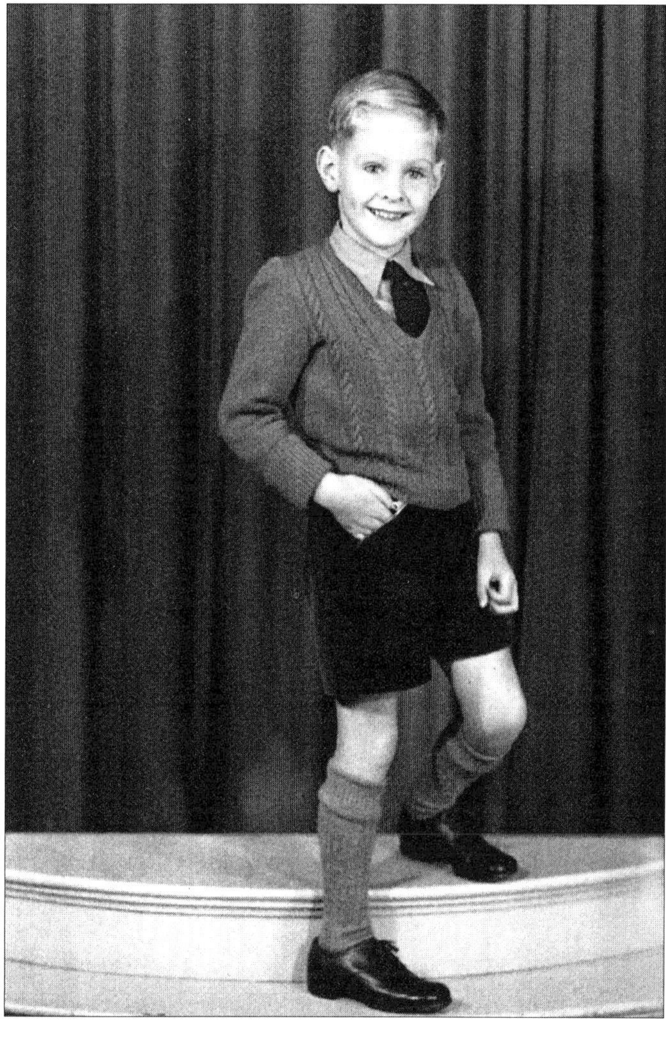

Fig 5 Portrait of a boy, *circa* 1952.

In other words, the memories made more accessible are those more compatible with the self-concept. Previous research shows that when exposure to emotionally arousing photographs intervenes between past events and retrieval, the findings include higher levels of retrieval (Anderson, Wais and Gabrieli 2006) or interference with the accuracy of recall (Deffenbacher, Bornstein and Penrod 2006). Consequently, we can be surer about the comprehensiveness of recounted memories with than without photo-elicitation but less certain about their accuracy.

In conclusion, the general model provides a means to organize knowledge, ideas, and insights about emotive factors that help make photographs memorable. Its building blocks include psychological theories of meaning, emotion, and memory established half-a-century or more ago that continue to endure and evolve with continued empirical testing. The new research described in this article tests one set of predictions from this model, with findings that replicate trends found in earlier research, clarify inconsistency in earlier conclusions and advance knowledge gained through empirical demonstration. The general model not only contains an implicit agenda for programmatic research on the psychology of photography, but an interdisciplinary blueprint to help integrate thinking about psychological factors that affect the reception to photographs across the spectrum of social sciences and humanities.

References

Anderson, A. K., Wais, P. E. and Gabrieli, J. D. 2006. Emotion Enhances Remembrance of Neutral Events Past. *Proceeding of the National Academy of Sciences, USA* 103(5): 1599–604.

Atkinson, R. C. and Shiffrin, R. M. 1968. Human Memory: A Proposed System and its Control Processes. In K. W. Spence and J. T. Spence (eds), *The Psychology of Learning and Motivation, vol. 8*. London: Academic Press.

Axelsson O. 2007. Towards a Psychology of Photography: Dimensions Underlying Aesthetic Appeal of Photographs. *Perceptual and Motor Skills* 105(2): 411–34.

Baddeley, A. D. 2000. The Episodic Buffer: A New Component of Working Memory? *Trends in Cognitive Science* 4: 417–23.

Bartlett, F. 1932. *Remembering*. Cambridge: Cambridge University Press.

Bradley, M. M., Codispoti, M., Sabatinelli, D. and Lang, P. J. 2001. Emotion and Motivation II: Sex Differences in Picture Processing. *Emotion* 1(3): 300–19.

Bradley, M. M., Greenwald, M. K., Petry, M. C. and Lang, P. J. 1992. Remembering Pictures: Pleasure and Arousal in Memory. *Journal of Experimental Psychology* 18(2): 379–90.

Bradley, M. M., Hamby, S., Löw, A. and Lang, P. J. 2007. Brain Potentials in Perception: Picture Complexity and Emotional Arousal. *Psychophysiology* 44(3): 364–73.

Christianson, S. A. and Fällman, L. 1990. The Role of Age on Reactivity and Memory for Emotional Pictures. *Scandanavian Journal of Psychology* 31(4): 291–301.

Cisler, J. M., Bacon, A. K. and Williams, N. L. 2009[2007]. Phenomenological Characteristics of Attentional Biases Towards Threat: A Critical Review. *Cognitive Therapy and Research* 33(2): 221–234. First published online in 2007.

Corr, P. J. 2008. Reinforcement Sensitivity Theory (RST): Introduction. In P. J. Corr (ed.), *The Reinforcement Sensitivity Theory of Personality*. Cambridge: Cambridge University Press.

Craik, F. I. M. and Lockhart, R. S. 1972. Levels of Processing: A Framework for Memory Research. *Journal of Verbal Learning and Verbal Behavior* 11: 671–84.

Deffenbacher, K. A., Bornstein, B. H. and Penrod, S. D. 2006. Mugshot Exposure Effects: Retroactive Interference, Mugshot Commitment, Source Confusion, and Unconscious Transference. *Law and Human Behaviour* 30(3): 287–307.

Greenberg, J., Pyszczynski, T., Solomon, S., Simon, L. and Breus, M. 1994. Role of Consciousness and Accessibility of Death-related Thoughts in Mortality Salience Effects. *Journal of Personality and Social Psychology* 67: 627–37.

Harper, D. 2002. Talking about Pictures: A Case for Photo-elicitation. *Journal of Visual Studies* 17: 13–26.

Heise, D. R. 2001. Project Magellan: Collecting Cross-cultural Affective Meanings via the Internet. *Electronic Journal of Sociology*. Available at http://www.sociology.org/content/vol005.003/mag.html.

James, W. 1890. *The Principles of Psychology*. 2 vols. New York: Henry Holt & Co.

Johnston, E. B. 2001. The Repeated Reproduction of Bartlett's Remembering. *History of Psychology* 4(4): 341–66.

Junghofer, M., Bradley, M. M., Elbert, T. R. and Lang, P. J. 2001. Fleeting Images: A New Look at Early Emotional Discrimination. *Psychophysiology* 38: 175–8.

Keenan, C. 1998. On the Relationship between Personal Photographs and Individual Memory. *History of Photography* 22(1): 60–4.

Koster, E. H. W., Crombez, G., Veschuere, B. and De Houwer, J. 2006. Attention to Threat in Anxiety-prone Individuals: Mechanisms Underlying Attentional Bias. *Cognitive Therapy and Research* 30(5): 635–43.

Landau, M. J., Greenberg, J., Solomon, S., Pyszczynzki, T. and Martens, A. 2006. Windows into Nothingness: Terror Management, Meaninglessness, and Negative Reactions to Modern Art. *Journal of Personality and Social Psychology*, 90(6): 879–92.

Lang, P. J., Bradley, M. M. aand Cuthbert, B. N. 1997. *International Affective Picture System (IAPS): Technical Manual and Affective Ratings*. Gainsville, FL: University of Florida.

Langford, M. 2008. Strange Bedfellows: Appropriations of the Vernacular by Photographic Artists. *Photography and Culture* 1(1): 73–94.

Mills, K. 2001. Making Meaning Brings Pleasure: The Influence of Titles on Aesthetic Experiences. *Emotion* 1: 320–9.

Nora, P. 2002. The Reasons for the Current Upsurge in Memory, *Transit – Europäische Revue* 22. Available at http://www.iwm.at/index. php?option=com_contentandtask=viewandid= 285andItemid=463.

Osgood, C. E., Suci, G. and Tannenbaum, P. H. 1967. *The Measurement of Meaning*. Urbana, IL: University of Illinois Press.

Osgood, C. E., May, W. H. and Miron, M. S. 1975. *Cross-Cultural Universals of Affective Meaning*. Urbana, IL: University of Illinois Press.

Potter, M. C. 1976. Short-term Conceptual Memory for Pictures. *Journal of Experimental Psychology Human Learning and Memory* 2(5): 509–22.

Rawlings, D. 2003. Personality Correlates of Liking for 'Unpleasant' Paintings and Photographs. *Personality and Individual Differences* 34(3): 395–410.

Rogers, C. R. 1947. Some Observations on the Organization of Personality. *American Psychologist*, 2: 358–68.

Rosenblatt, A., Greenberg, J., Solomon, S., Pyszczynski, T. and Lyon, D. 1989. Evidence for Terror Management Theory I: The Effects of Mortality Salience on Reactions to Those who Violate or Uphold Cultural Values. *Journal of Personality and Social Psychology* 57: 681–90.

Russell, P. A. 2003. Effort after Meaning and the Hedonic Value of Paintings. *British Journal of Psychology* 94: 99–110.

Sánchez-Navarro, J. P., Martínez-Selva, J. M., Román, F. and Ginesa, T. 2006. The Effect of Content and Physical Properties of Affective Pictures on Emotional Responses. *Spanish Journal of Psychology* 9(2): 145–53.

Sharot, T. and Phelps, E. A. 2004. How Arousal Modulates Memory: Disentangling the Effects of Attention and Retention *Cognitive, Affective and Behavioral Neuroscience* 4(3): 294–306.

Sontag. S. 1977. *On Photography*. London: Penguin.

Staal, M. A. 2004. *Stress, Cognition, and Human Performance: A Literature Review and Conceptual Framework*. NASA/TM—2004-212824. Available at http://humanfactors.arc.nasa.gov/web/library/ publications/publications.php.

Sturken, M. 1999. The Image as Memorial: Personal Photographs in Cultural Memory. In M. J. Hirsch (ed.), *The Familial Gaze*. Lebanon, NH: University Press of New England.

Tuller, M. and Pinto, J. 2005. Effects of Anxiety on Attention and Visual Memory. *Journal of Vision* 5(8): 389–9a.

Valentine, T. and Mesout, J. 2009[2008]. Eyewitness Identification under Stress in the London Dungeon. *Applied Cognitive Psychology* 23(2): 151–161. Originally published online in 2008.

**Photography
& Culture**

Volume 2—Issue 2
July 2009
pp. 135–152
DOI:
10.2752/175145109X12456654102722

Reprints available directly
from the publishers

Photocopying permitted by
licence only

The Lure of Discipline: Military Aesthetics and the Making of the First World War Civilian Soldier

Jane Tynan

Jane Tynan is a cultural studies lecturer at Central Saint Martins College of Art and Design, University of the Arts London. She recently completed her PhD thesis on First World War British military uniform which considers its role in the construction of the wartime male body. The research explores the formation of meaning of army clothing through representations, personal experiences, production processes, trade sources and official regulations. From this research she has contributed a book chapter to *British Popular Culture and the First World War* (2008). Her research interests include social histories of clothing and design in early twentieth century modernity.

Abstract

Much research on the British experience of the First World War relies on literary accounts. This article looks instead to the role of press photographs in constructing a popular discourse of the wartime male body. Sequenced body movements used in official training manuals, were taken up enthusiastically by the weekly and daily press in 1914 to promote active service among the British public. Narratives of bio-political control became prevalent as the war found men's bodies increasingly viewed an official resource. On the pages of popular newspapers, the language of military discipline enacted the visual transformation of civilians to working soldiers. It is clear that press images of recruit training, used to unite public opinion during the First World War, were inspired by the uniformity of military discipline. This article explores how these photographs worked in the context of a whole discourse that aestheticized the military body. It not only draws attention to a wartime visual culture that supported a project of collective discipline but offers insights into why the politics of militarized display troubled later debates about the representation of servicemen in public war remembrance.

Keywords: Military aesthetics, uniform, discourse, collective discipline, transformation, mass mobilisation

> It is discipline mainly which distinguishes a regiment of soldiers from a crowd of men.
>
> Captain E. John Solano, *Drill and Field Training*

Whether images of war create myths or reflect experience, they invariably invoke the figure of the soldier. Unlike soldiers' literary narratives of the First World War, which offered images of bodies in pieces (Tate 1998), early press photographs sought versions of the male body that echoed the discipline of official army manuals. Over 700,000 British soldiers were killed, many bodies went unrecovered, but those who returned bore the visible marks of an adventure gone wrong. If the realities of mutilation and disfigurement meant the conflict signaled a crisis for the male body (Bourke 1996; Cole 2003), the image of the soldier became a site for the struggle between myth and experience.

Literature may act as witness to the modernism of wartime myth making (Fussell 1975; Hynes 1990; Tate 1998) but visual and material aspects of wartime culture also show a remarkable capacity for illusion. This paper considers not only popular illusions of specific kinds of wartime

photographs but their singular concern with the aesthetics of military discipline. If portrait photographs taken of soldiers during the war evoked their individual humanity *behind* the uniform (Moriarty 2003: 40), press photographs sought to express citizenship *through* the uniform. War experience might have shattered these illusions but the desire for homogeneity was reflected in the way the aesthetics of military discipline became part of the visual culture of war. It has been argued that the visibility of collective disciplines on the pages of wartime illustrated newspapers was often at the expense of collective action (Wombell 1986). Only those conforming to the war effort appeared on its pages. This paper considers how photographic images echoed the concerns of army training manuals; both located military strength in the wartime male body as an effect of discipline; both promised to transform civilians to soldiers. If bodies later become an emblem for war memory it was mass slaughter that brought their fragility into focus. However, early in the war if men's bodies appeared robust it was because editors of the weekly and daily press shared the optimism of Herbert Horatio Kitchener who wanted to create a mass volunteer army by getting as many civilians as possible into khaki.

Starting in August 1914 on the western front as a war of movement, both sides in the First World War were by the end of that year caught in the trench system. By November the retreat from Mons and the first battle of Ypres had decimated the original British army but by the end of October Kitchener issued a call for 300,000 volunteers in anticipation of a war of attrition. The response was to open the channels of supply of men and goods to win the war. *The War Illustrated* ran a story in early November 1914, "Turning Young Patriots into Trained Fighting-men" (7 November, 1914: 289), which reflected the growing concern about the supply shortage of volunteers by showing keen recruits in mufti already holding rifles. This image of thirty men in synchronized movement was followed by a photograph of recruits taking cover behind the boards of a polo ground. On the bottom left-hand corner of the page men are shown engaged in bayonet practice, and in the last photograph uniformed recruits lie in trenches dug out in a training field. Order and uniformity are suggested in these photographs not only by the presentation of men forming neat lines but by the way their bodies fade into the background, as if replicated into infinity.

Almost certainly staged for the camera, these maneuvers in wartime press photographs offer an insight into what was thought to make a good soldier in 1914. Emphasis in military history on the efficiency of systematic drill, a Roman model adopted to make armed action semi-automatic (Lyon 1994: 27), shows the practical value placed on uniform appearance. Over five images, *The War Illustrated* uses the spectacle of drill to construct soldiering as automated. Like the "instrumental realism" of the industrial photograph discussed by Allan Sekula (1986), the medium appears to transform civilians through military disciplines, but also creates illusions of durability by mechanizing soldiers' bodies. Measurement, synchronization and mechanical reproduction support of the idea of war as machine (Pick 1993: 165–188) and in the early twentieth century the fantasy of the machine aesthetic in visual culture gave

the impression that the body of the soldier could be "assembled."

Joanna Bourke argues in her study on the changing shape of men's bodies in wartime Britain that an official discourse emerged about the male body which viewed its health and fitness part of the national economy (Bourke 1996: 30). As the Munitions of War Act in July 1915 tackled problems of manpower resourcing, concerns about the military became a national problem, which drew attention to the fitness of the male body for military participation. In wartime Britain, the appetite for authentic, close-up images was so great that photographs were generated specifically to feed it, and many papers started as a direct result of the war (*Mitchell's Press Directory* 1914). The Boer War established the newspaper as conduit between battle and home front and the development of the mass-circulation newspaper during the Boer War showed the press that war sold newspapers (Farrar 1998: 6). While the official propaganda requirements of the Boer War stimulated the consumption of popular military objects, the First World War saw the production and consumption of many new products (Paris 2000: 136–8). The rituals of military life were not so new to the vast majority of working-class and lower-middle class readers already culturally conditioned for war (Clark 1996: 38–53). A popular culture complicit with patriotic militarism was powerful, contributing to the enlistment of 300,000 men in August 1914 and by the end of the year a further 700,000 (Winter 1985: 30). By this time, distinctions between "military" and "civilian" were breaking down making popular opinion an important strategic resource (Dandeker 1990: 104). In this context, newspapers became a significant source of propaganda to mobilize men to war.

Despite the failure to provide decent clothing, adequate weaponry or indeed living space, images of military discipline, control and order persisted in the press. The war readiness sought in recruits, however, had not yet been achieved by army authorities. Confusion arose precisely due to distinctions between recruitment and enlistment. The British army could get men to join but frequently had problems with recording details, medical examining and training (Silbey 2005). While the authorities struggled to clothe and equip new recruits, images of military perfection continued to be used to attract men to join the army. Indeed, images of discipline appeared critical to the creation of a civilian army. These photographs of civilians conforming to military discipline recall John Tagg's view of the institutional uses of photographs (Tagg 1988). Their role is not to witness history but create it. As a 1911 training manual stated, discipline was taking on new meanings linked to body efficiency: "In the field, discipline no longer consists of rigid obedience, but of that quick and orderly motion which results from permanent organization and training; that knowledge that the mass will act as a unit" (Fuller 1911: 42). This discourse viewed the body as a kind of moving image, a focus for collective disciplines and a place to locate fantasies of military power.

Pictures found a role in newspaper publishing when the *Illustrated London News* emerged in the 1840s to record "historic events" (Martin 2006: 19–21). In the mid-1800s editors became convinced of the pedagogical benefits of illustrated accounts of the war, which met the popular desire

for "historical spectacle" (Sekula 1999: 188) during a war subject to unprecedented levels of news management. Filmmakers and photographers explored war themes that drew on realism and the preparation of the body became a popular theme when films used scenes behind the lines, training and life of the troops, inspections and drill (Low 1973: 155). However, limitations of censorship meant that only certain kinds of photographs reached the illustrated press and it was only by 1916 that the first official British photographers were established on the western front (Carmichael 1989: 47). Images of drill were the result of restrictions to battlefront action and many photographs were staged to supply the growing illustrated press. Pre-1916 restrictions on access to battlefields forced photographers to improvise, so news of the war often came in the form of images of anonymous soldiers "getting prepared" (Carmichael 1989; Lewinski 1978).

One such feature appeared In *The Sphere* in November 1914 when supply of manpower ran low in the army, called "The Recruit: How he is trained through the early stages of a soldier's career" (November 14, 1914: 170–1), which depicted volunteers making the passage from civilian to soldier once "fitted out with clothing and other regimental necessaries" (November 14, 1914: 170–1). From the civilian men at the recruiting tents in Whitehall to the officers lining up for inspection at Lincoln's Inn, men's minds and bodies appear altered by exposure to a range of army practices. As Michel Foucault argued, modern institutions use disciplinary techniques to transform and control bodies: "The human body was entering a machinery of power that explores it, breaks it down and rearranges it" (Foucault 1991: 138). By entering an army system the recruit was shown submitting his body to rearrangement, a process described by newspaper narratives that explored and broke it down. Thus, popular newspapers were part of the national project to rearrange the civilian male body according to military interests.

This photographic discourse used images of soldiers "getting prepared" to promote military participation. While there are many photographs of the conflict, no single war photographer emerges and mundane subject matter (Lewinski 1978) suggests they were largely created in the national interest. These photographs show soldiers augmented by military objects and perfected by military discipline. The growth of individualism meant that participation in any national project was invited through the "freedom to be a consumer within a growing industrialised Britain" (Curran 1978: 72). Thus, the body was presented in popular culture as a project, to be rearranged and transformed by material objects. Military discipline was no exception. Indeed, if nineteenth-century illustrated newspapers "… contributed to the construction of collective imaginaries and to the production of cultural commodities" (Martin 2006: 50) these wartime periodicals made militarism appear an ideal form of citizenship.

"Discipline is Instinctive Knowledge"

Foucault's work on bio-politics in the late twentieth century shifted thinking about political power from territory to population. Foucault saw power as productive and the body a focus of institutional reform. When

concerns were raised before the war about the state of the nation, men's bodies were singled out for attention. As General Ian Hamilton stated in a 1913 army manual, "Military training is giving definite shape to a sense of citizenship now vague and formless" (Hamilton 1913: 81). Clearly, his desire to re-cast men's bodies as soldiers was part of a wider social project based on military discipline. His vision of militarized civilians valued the role of army training to observably improve the body, in line with Foucault's critique of modern institutions. "The exercise of discipline presupposes a mechanism that coerces by means of observation" (Foucault 1991: 170) shows how a disciplinary structure based on observation replaced traditional strategies of corporal punishment (Foucault 1991). Indeed, Foucault began by describing this changing political economy of the body through changing conceptions of the soldier, which found its modern form an ideal achieved through training: "the soldier has become something that can be made" (Foucault 1991: 135).

Corporeal inscription was a recurrent theme for popular press stories during wartime, which chimed with beliefs about military discipline found in army training manuals: "Discipline, according to von Moltke, should result from a good military education the end of which is solely to cause it to pass into the flesh and blood. In this sense discipline is instinctive knowledge" (Fuller 1914: 74). Force of habit was thought to discipline the civilian body. If a normalizing gaze made surveillance critical to the inscription of social bodies, so long as recruits were subject to reform and education, they could be disciplined by the inculcation of habit. As both army manuals and press images suggest, comporting the body differently appeared to be the basis for militarizing the civilian body. Another wartime training manual saw the control of men's movements key to military discipline: "The object of drills by numbers is to teach men to perform each separate motion of every movement correctly … Uniformity is arrived at by training each man to act at the right time and in the right manner on any given word of command" (Solano 1915: 20). In terms of military organization, this suggests the visual construction of the soldier's body was a technique of army discipline. Visual codes, according to Foucault, are not just surface detail but are bound up in creative and purposeful disciplinary technologies. Body training enabled the military unit to function but images of recruit training actually visualized the process of breaking down each movement to describe how uniform behavior could be crafted.

Newspaper images of civilians getting prepared for war were, therefore, critical to the cultural conditioning of the body politic for mass voluntary enlistment. By multiplying the venues where soldiers' bodies could be observed, mass mobilization found support in a popular visual culture, which viewed the male body as an object of public interest (Bourke 1996). Further, central to the movement for national efficiency, the human body was the focus for a science of improvement of the "national physique" (Searle 2003: 64). Such were popular beliefs about the role of military discipline in transforming civilians that, when Kitchener's improvised blue uniforms failed to accentuate the body, drill was used to show the strength of military stock. Faced with the

disappointing sight of badly dressed soldiers Rudyard Kipling's description emphasized their physicality:

> They were clad in a blue garb that disguised all contours; yet their shoulders, backs, and loins could not altogether be disguised, and these were excellent. Another company, at physical drill in shirt and trousers, showed what superb material had offered itself to be worked upon, and how much poise and directed strength had been added to that material in the past few months. (Kipling 1915: 5–6)

Kipling's description of the new recruits reflected official views that civilian bodies were material and the success of army training lay in their improvement. The photographic cells of press stories invited readers into the army training camp by documenting visual narratives of improvement and transformation. If mass recruitment demanded public interest in preparations of the military body, exposing the means of its production was designed to encourage military participation. Military and social interests converged in this wartime project to discipline the British male body.

If discipline and control, physicality and exposure to risk distinguished military from civilian life, it is clear why the "theater of war" was officially viewed a site for shaping hegemonic masculinities (Morgan 1994: 168). The *Illustrated War News* carried a story in December 1914 that presented an anonymous soldier's body in a diagram on the carrying and handling of rifle-grenades. "As used by the British Against the German Trenches almost touching their own: Rifle-Grenades" (December 2, 1914: 46) uses a visual narrative to show the effectiveness of British rifle-grenades through numbered frames that draw readers around each episode in sequence. Readers interpolated by the apparent objectivity of the analysis were invited to view science as a solution to the problem of the body. Uniform and weaponry enhance an image of automated masculinity, to suggest that the battlefield is the ideal place to become a man. On the left-hand side, the first photograph depicts a carrier holding three grenades, cartridges for firing them with detonators and rope for throwing by hand. In the second, uniformed soldiers are carefully lined up in a trench equipped with fire grenades. While the third view faces the soldier's back as four grenades are carried on his waist belt, views four, five and six show the grenade and demonstrate one fixed for firing. The photographs mechanize the soldier by aligning body movements with actions required for use of weaponry, to suggest a body created for battlefield tasks. This is this sense in which the soldier is presented, in Foucault's terms, as something that can be made.

If military success were viewed in terms of industrial production and scientific innovation, images of soldiers were increasingly charged with technological value and their physicality exploited for propagandist purposes. Anson Rabinach has argued that a scientific approach to the working body emerging in the late nineteenth century gained currency in the twentieth century, which saw the widespread use of the metaphor of the human motor to describe the human body (Rabinbach 1992). In the military context, these capacities were visualized by images of mechanized bodies, disciplined by drill routines, uniform behavior and dress. By emphasizing the role

of visual and material practices to produce the military body, images of military discipline might have promised the volunteer an improved body for combat, but weaponry was also regularly exhibited in the popular press to advertise British technological prowess. The war effort was not just about supplying men for battle but also meant a contest in industrial production.

In the press stories discussed, the camera closely supervised soldiers' actions, divided and atomized by the individual cells of the photographic frame. Thus, these layouts shaped not just the construction but also the interpretation of popular narratives about army life. Historically linked to official forms of classification and surveillance, photographs were routinely used as documentary evidence to prompt health, security and social reforms (Tagg 1988). Here they contrive to document the life of the civilian soldier, as if narrating the transformative effects of military discipline. As John Tagg argues, following Foucault, photography generated knowledge to became a tool of power that "… could find a new metaphor in the unobtrusive cells of the photographic frame; in its ever more minute division of time and motion; in its ever finer scrutiny of bodies in stringent laboratory conditions" (Tagg 1988: 87). Like Eadward Muybridge's catalog of body movements, the camera appears to manage the body of the soldier by obsessively recording the minutest detail in movement. Later, photographs were used for time and motion studies, especially "micro-motion studies" by followers of Taylorism, influenced by the photographs of Muybridge (Warner Marien 2006).

By following the movements of the the soldier's body, the camera exploited the aesthetics of military discipline. Beside the concrete role of science and technology in fighting the war lay a symbolic role that called on discourses of industrial production to fortify the soldier's body in the field and describe how a strong civilian army might be built. If, as Sekula argues, criminal identification photographs were, in the late nineteenth century, designed to facilitate arrest (Sekula 1986: 7) then these wartime photographs facilitated not just recruitment but dramatized enlistment. Discipline, as stated in the 1915 British army manual *Drill and Field Training*, created soldiers from civilians. These photographs, and the way they are chronicled describes enlistment as a journey of the body. In press photographs and official army manuals narratives of transformation from civilian to soldier were presented in different ways. In both venues, images of discipline symbolized corporeal transformation.

As uniformed soldiers were a source of entertainment throughout the 1800s, the requirements of military spectacle were often given more importance than military training (Myerly 1996: 139–65). By the twentieth century, representational modes emerged capable of incorporating military spectacle into an official agenda that shaped mass culture. Wartime censorship and news management reflected the different ways in which the press had to conform to military authorities from 1914 to 1918. Many competing official demands called for careful management of information on the war, which in many cases resulted in the absence of "hard news." The two regulations in the Defence of the Realm Act (DORA) relevant to censorship were regulation 18 and regulation 27; the latter made it an

offence among other things to "spread false reports" or "prejudice recruiting" resulting in restrictions on publication (Gregory 2004: 22). Despite this, however, most newspaper editors were willing to use their papers to support government policy (Marquis 1978: 476). This was not always in the form of overt propaganda or the direct result of censorship but after 12 November 1914, when Stanley Buckmaster took over as Director of the Press Bureau, it was established that publication could not assist the enemy, disclose the movement of troops or "unduly depress our people" (Lovelace 1978: 311). While this approach may have initially reassured the public that they would be spared the worst details, as the war progressed it deprived them of news at the front. Indeed, adopting a repressive policy presented problems, especially for recruiting. The challenge for editors was how to do their patriotic duty, satisfy a public hungry for news of the war while operating within a restrictive environment (Lovelace 1978: 317).

Despite serious restrictions on news, the health of newspaper publishing was widely recognized at the start of the First World War. Increased consumption of newspapers in the late nineteenth and early twentieth century may have been traditionally linked to general improvements in literacy but Raymond Williams argues that as literacy rates were far ahead of newspaper reading (Williams 1978: 42) it was instead the way newspaper stories incorporated established popular forms in the emphasis on "crime, adventure and spectacle" which gave them wide appeal (Williams 1978: 45). The British press in the early twentieth century consisted of a wide variety of publications and as newspaper buying increased, structure and ownership contracted to fewer participants to eliminate the residual presence of radicalism. Stories may have drawn on established popular forms but by the war were characterized by conformity, and many newspapers sought a visual language to promote an imperialist and nationalist view (Curran 1978: 72). Representations of soldiers were part of that popular culture and the role of newspapers in dramatizing transformations from civilian to working soldier reflected the extent to which newspaper editors were prepared to act in the national interest.

The way images were deployed in these periodicals offers some insight into how soldiers were visually constructed for the British public, particularly as many British illustrated periodicals formed part of the national press. Photographs took up most of the space in illustrated wartime papers, which were accompanied by captions. *The War Illustrated*, *The Illustrated War News* and *The Sphere* were weeklies and part of the magazine market while a newspaper publisher owned *The Daily Mirror* which became a picture paper. The successful periodical *The War Illustrated* was published throughout the 1914–18 conflict, to appeal to the working classes and relied in the first part of the war on sensationalism; entire pages featured six or more photographs per page, each usually on a single theme or subject. British publishers, keen on these specialist news magazines that dealt specifically with war news, also developed *The Illustrated War News* for a more prosperous middle-class market. It contained quality photographs as well as drawings and used various sepia tones, good-quality paper and avoided sensationalism, appealing instead

to readers' desire for improvement. The *Daily Mirror*, before the First World War a very successful newspaper, found circulation figures rose during the war. Selling at a halfpenny, this illustrated morning paper had in 1910 circulation figures of 900,000, rising to 1,000,000 just before the war and roughly 1,200,000 by 1914 (McEwan 1982: 459–86). Indeed, the success of this paper during the war lay in the wartime move in the newspaper market to the tabloid in response to a growing demand for news in pictures (McEwan 1982: 479–81). Established in 1903, by July 1916 the *Daily Mirror* sales reached 1,307,000 and it was the first picture paper to sell for half a penny (McEwan 1982: 482).

On the other end of the scale the sixpenny weekly *The Sphere* was an upmarket periodical equally reliant on images of war and established in 1900 to report on the war in South Africa (*Mitchell's Newspaper Press Directory* 1914). This varied illustrated press reached a range of social groups and supplied them with news of war in visual form. As these popular newspapers advanced an official agenda, recruitment campaigns were clearly bolstered by their presentation of soldiers quickly and easily conforming to army discipline. In wartime periodicals, visual narratives relied upon the realism and documentary appeal of photography to make bodily transformation appear plausible. It did not matter for which social group stories were made. In the daily and weekly illustrated press, men's bodies were idealized and produced by the visual symbols of military discipline: drill and uniform. Photographs were particularly suitable to document narratives of body improvement and transformation, revealing discipline as a visual effect that automated men's movements. Indeed, the photograph could use the body to exploit the aesthetics of military discipline, especially when uniformity indicated regulation and control of the civilian body.

Military Precision and Mass-production

As military organization grew from the eighteenth century, it anticipated the industrial age of "total war" in the twentieth century, which deployed the soldier's body in specific ways: "One symbol of the new discipline of precision drill was the introduction of the uniform … ensuring that the soldier subsumed his identity beneath that of the military organisation" (Dandeker 1990: 70). Uniform became increasingly important to military organization as one of the range of techniques used to discipline the body of the soldier. As already argued, images of uniformity and body control were central to convey a popular militarism on the home front during the First World War. What uniformity was expected to do for internal military discipline, it was during this war doing for collective national discipline. A focus on the outward details of the body meant the army could detect deviation and fault through the observation of patterns of behavior. By popularizing military discipline, illustrated newspapers reflected the official national agenda of mass mobilization through collective discipline.

A 1913 army manual emphasized how attention to the appearance of the body encourages discipline: "The outward and visible signs of the compulsory cadet system I place in the following order. Discipline,

self-restraint, good manners, cleanliness, physical development, some useful military aptitudes …" (Hamilton 1913: 48). The army system relied on corporeal inscription, in particular the careful arrangement of outward appearance, to discipline recruits, as bodily uniformity was highly suggestive of military appearance. In 1915, a newspaper feature used photographs of recruits' synchronized movements in drill training on Hampstead Heath in London. Despite the continued high level of volunteering, by January 1915 there were increased manpower demands from the war office. "Swedish Drill Aided by Street-railings: The Queen Victoria Rifles Exercising near Jack Straw's Castle at Hampstead" appeared in *The Illustrated War News* using the aesthetics of military precision to show the mass-militarizing of civilians on the home front (January 13, 1915: 30) (Figure 1).

At the time Swedish drill was favored by the British army, a free-standing communal exercise in direct response to a series of commands given to a definite order, which built up a toned body and replaced the traditional emphasis on muscularity (Bourke 1996: 180). Indeed, drill was advocated by the war office as a technique for producing the disciplined soldier as a 1914 infantry training manual conveys: "Drill in close order is of first importance in producing discipline, cohesion, and the habits of absolute and instant obedience to the orders of a superior" (War Office 1914: 3). Drill routines might have been designed to encourage obedience but drill orders made particularly striking images in popular culture. Four images of drill training show the same large group of men in public performing the maneuvers using park railings as bars. An

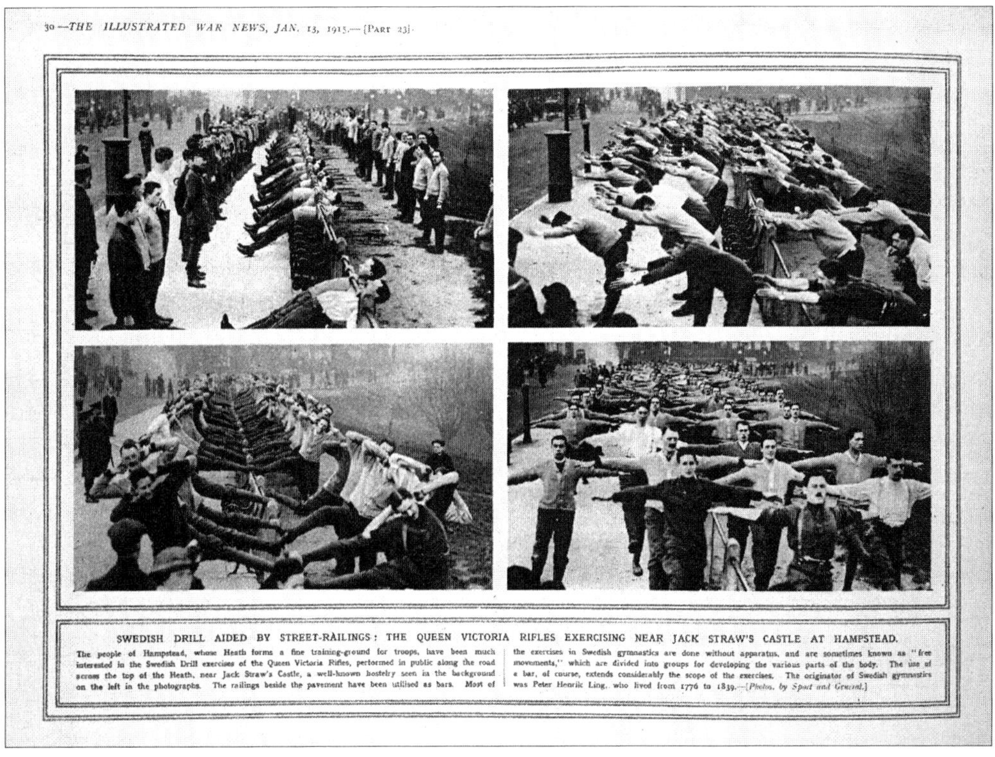

Fig 1 "Swedish Drill Aided by Street-railings: The Queen Victoria Rifles Exercising near Jack Straw's Castle at Hampstead." *Illustrated War News*, January 13, 1915, p. 30.

automated body, celebrated in this image of recruit-training on Hampstead Heath, saw military and social interests converge in the fit male body conforming to military discipline. In the first photograph most of the recruits look on as a group of men practice Swedish drill, while the second shows the full group practicing free movements where they push their bodies forward in unison. In the next photograph they are shown resting one leg on the rails while the last depicts them in another free movement with outstretched arms fixing their gaze straight ahead at the camera.

An army training camp improvised from civilian leisure space presents military discipline as part of a wider social project. The visual effect of uniformity on Hampstead Heath heightens the sense that volunteers were enlisted to the military project through the alteration of their habits and rearrangement of their bodies. Indeed, if uniformity gives this mass of bodies a reassuring visual symmetry it is due to the way disciplinary techniques are exploited to create the appearance of an army manufactured from a crowd of men. As a regimental history describes, the visual impact of new recruits was taken as proof of their latent military strength, detected by the author through the pride they were willing to take in their appearance: "There was something hidden in those youths which was to come out in the training. The spirit of the soldier was only dormant. Rough diamonds all; only waiting to be polished to show their worth … I saw them swinging along before they had their khaki already taking pride in their appearance" (Rimmer 1917: 8–9). During wartime, too much pride taken in civilian appearance was frowned upon (Ugolini 2007: 71–98), making patriots of men who wanted to look like soldiers.

The lure of discipline was a powerful wartime fantasy. It invested in the perceived beauty of hegemonic masculinities forged in open spaces in preparation for the battlefield. This was the fantasy of the civilian body made durable by military discipline, advanced by a popular visual culture that blurred the lines between entertainment and reality. Foucault's view of discipline as productive power accounts for the pleasure taken in images of body uniformity in wartime: "In his view, discipline is a productive power par excellence: it aims not only to constrain those over who it is exercised, but also to enhance and make use of their capacities" (Hindess 1996: 113). John Tagg argued that images exist as part of "a systematic photographic discourse" (Tagg 1988) to enforce ideologies and versions of history. If recruits' bodies were routinely presented in newspapers undergoing transformations, whether through narratives of training or dressing, then military aesthetics became part of a discourse of discipline that encouraged men into army life.

These newspaper photographs show recruits transformed by disciplinary techniques. This ideal of military spectacle fits Foucault's conception of a modernity that introduced clean, rational forms of social control, replacing the disorderly crowd with "… a collection of separated individualities" (Foucault 1991: 201). Like many stories in the illustrated press, military spectacle atomized bodies, just as each photograph is a cell to trap the body for observation. In his discussion of the iconography of the First World War, Paul Fussell argued that uniformity was a modern aesthetic, of which the Field Service Postcard was part, a metaphor for practices associated with standardization and uniformity (Fussell 1975: 186). The postcard, a form letter sent to the relatives of those killed or injured during battle was, as Fussell explained, a "form" capable of "Infinite replication and utter uniformity" (Fussell 1975: 186). This utopian view of the endless reproducibility of postcards is haunted by the sinister notion that men's bodies too were part of a similar production-line aesthetic.

"Soldier-Making at Express-Speed"

As uniformed institutions became more prevalent in the late 1800s (De Marly 1986), Britain was marked by increased state intervention (Tickner 2000: 190), which spread uniformity from military to state institutions. A recurring theme in the iconography of the First World War, uniformity could also be linked with the development of techniques for mass-production. A key theme in the modernization of European societies at the end of the nineteenth century, uniformity drove the standardization of time, which eased the smooth working of political, economic, scientific and legal operations (Kern 1983: 12). Further, A. J. P. Taylor argued that uniform time allowed the development of pre-1914 mobilization timetables that led to the outbreak of war (Taylor 1969). For Gertrude Stein, the First World War was Cubist (Kern 1983: 287–318) and ultimately made modernism legible (Tate, 1998: 4). The celebration of uniformity in modernity extended to body projects. The leveling effect of the urban crowd, the introduction of uniform time and the experience of soldiers on the battlefield had a shared experience of simultaneity mediated by technology. Here, however, the production line expressed the way faith in progress was replaced by faith in production in the early twentieth century (Giedion 1948: 31). During this period a number of images used this production-line aesthetic. Whether depicting chorus girls, pupils or soldiers, themes of uniformity and replication extended to representations of the body in the popular press. In "A pillar of strength" found in *Daily Mirror* a group of boys formed a pillar while at gymnastic training at the naval training school at Elmham, East Anglia (16 March, 1916: 6). In *The Daily Mirror* "A Strenuous Holiday: Teachers taking a course of 'Eurhythmics'" schoolmistresses danced barefooted to music on a lawn, to form a neat orderly line of bodies (August 5, 1916: 6–7).

Pre-dating Kracauer's later schema of "The Mass Ornament," which he found in the extravagant spectacle of the Tiller Girls, a dance troupe in 1920s Berlin, these press stories made sense of the mass through a visual mechanization of the body: "The mass ornament is the aesthetic reflex of the rationality to which the prevailing economic

system aspires" (Kracauer 1995: 78–9). In their synchronized movements, soldiers appeared to form part of an automated system and, like the Tiller Girls' formations, a rational aesthetic. Foucault's "disciplinary society" uses the concept of a new technology of power/knowledge to show how discourse is implicated in strategies of power and domination (Foucault 1991). Photographs used in the illustrated press were part of a system of surveillance that saw transformative effects in the spectacle of military disciplines like systematic drill, outdoor exercising and putting on uniform.

Despite the fact that in peacetime a man required eleven months training from basic drill to divisional exercises, Kitchener 's optimism meant that this period was reduced to six months for the New Armies (Rawson 2006: 27). In March 1915, the *Daily Mirror* used visual uniformity to reflect that optimism and convey the efficiency of army training techniques. "Learning to Bayonet the Germans in their Trenches" showed recruits in training charging sacks with bayonets, in a mock German trench (March 25, 1915: 8–9) (Figure 2). Synchronized to appear semi-automatic, soldiers' movements supplied an ideal military spectacle, which exploited the physicality of army practices, to convey how discipline was applied to recruits. Army modernization was achieved through the adoption of military discipline through the co-ordination of units (Dandeker 1990: 69). Synchronized movement of soldiers appears to supply evidence of the success of military training but by 1915 enthusiasm for the war was on the decline and images were not convincing the home front. Later in the year the *Illustrated War News* carried a story that proposed a brief but effective transformation

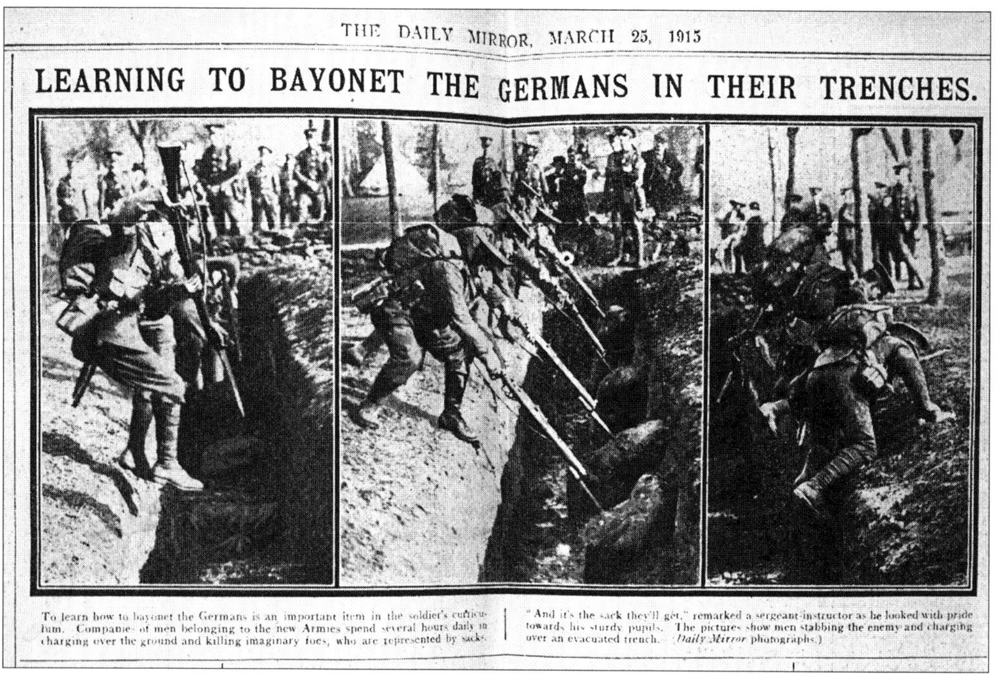

Fig 2 "Learning to Bayonet the Germans in their Trenches." *Daily Mirror* March 23, 1915, pp. 8–9.

from civilian to soldier. "Soldier-Making at Express Speed: From Recruit to Gunner under training in forty-five minutes" presented "soldier-making at express speed" through a series of four photographs that showed the hypothetical recruit transformed to gunner in forty-five minutes (September 22, 1915: 30). In the first image men in civilian dress gather at the door of a recruiting station, followed by one showing the same men being issued with uniforms. In the third, the men line up in full regulation dress for inspection, while the last shows them having their first gunnery lesson. The text not only describes how uniform constructs the soldier but describes body transformation: "As a method of attracting men, the secret of successful recruiting seems to be to put a recruit into uniform immediately he joins" (September 22, 1915: 30).

These kinds of stories continued after the Military Service Act of January 1916, a measure to increase manpower through conscription (Winter 1985: 28–40). However it was likely that a story in the *Daily Mirror* at the end of January 1916 (January 24, 1916: 3) referred to a form of volunteering called the Derby Scheme. "Quick Change for 'Derbyites'" showed approximately twenty men in civilian dress descending in a lift at army headquarters. The second photograph finds the same men once again ascending in the lift dressed in uniform, "They returned seven minutes later dressed in khaki" (January

24, 1916: 3). Indeed, this quick change is represented not through a single photograph but a series of photographs to chronicle body transformation.

Uniformity was an observable ideal in military training as photographs in the popular press promoted surveillance practices described in official training literature. Clearly, the ideal outcome of disciplinary army practices was bodily uniformity, carefully constructed through a range of army practices. However, a photographic discourse emerged in the popular wartime press, which echoed the disciplines set out in official army literature that promoted work to the male body in wartime. When modern ideas about fashioning the body through exercise, adornment and grooming were gaining currency, these practices were harnessed not only to standardize and control the army recruit but to convey these processes to a wider public. Michèle Martin argues that war coverage, particularly suited to forming solidarity among different classes, used images but also industrial techniques and editorial control to give thematic presentation of stories homogeneity (Martin 2006: 238). The soldier's body became a focus in popular newspapers to unite people around images of collective discipline through observation of the soldier's body. By exploiting military aesthetics newspapers endlessly documented the construction of the ideal soldier as a civilian quickly conforming to army discipline.

It is clear that press images of recruit training, used to unite public opinion during the First World War, were inspired by the uniformity of military discipline. In photographs, uniform clothing aided the instrumentality of soldiers' bodies to signify the change that characterized the vital transformation from civilian to soldier. If clothing dramatizes images it is also suggestive of the gap between experience and myth. It is not surprising that conscientious objectors used the uniform as a focus for their resistance to military service. In visual culture, clothing plays the role of fantasy: of seduction, transformation and escape. In wartime, all of these fantasies were used in photographs that recruited civilians to khaki. Voluntary enlistment, stimulated by images of men in synchronized movement, forming neat lines, was a visual culture that returned a much desired order to the body. This imaginary order created by photographs might have been a defense against the mutilation and death that became the abiding story of the western front.

Such was public confidence in the national project of collective discipline that many of these popular images appeared to replicate the male body into infinity. However, these photographs are now haunted by a future promised but not delivered, a utopia instead replaced by the nightmare of slaughter. The truth they assert has been overtaken by images of war memory that either show bodies in pieces or avoid the problems of triumphant militarized display. Far from making these photographs redundant, their flawed logic makes these historical objects all the more compelling.

These photographs signify a defining moment in the story of the wartime male body. Viewed as a resource, men's bodies became objects for public scrutiny and photography was a medium that could be exploited for propaganda purposes. Photographs used by the weekly and daily press that proudly displayed bodies transformed by army discipline, represent a moment of belief in the mechanization of the body, a project in which neither photographers nor newspaper editors were innocent bystanders. First World War mass mobilization relied not only on science and technology but also on a popular culture that told stories of soldiers not born but made.

References

Barthes, Roland. 1977. *Image, Music, Text.* London: Fontana.

Becker, Karin E. 2002. Photojournalism and the Tabloid Press. In Liz Wells (ed.), *The Photography Reader.* London: Routledge.

Bourke, Joanna. 1996. *Dismembering the Male: Men's Bodies, Britain and the Great War.* London: Reaktion Books.

Brothers, Caroli. 1997. *War and Photography: A Cultural History.* London: Routledge.

Carmichael, Jane. 1989. *First World War Photographers.* London: Routledge

Clark, Lloyd. 1996. "Civilians Entrenched": The British Home Front and Attitudes to the First World War, 1914–18. In Ian Stewart and Susan L. Carruthers (eds), *War, Culture and the Media. Representations of the Military in Twentieth Century Britain.* London: Flicks Books.

Cole, Sarah. 2003. *Modernism, Male Friendship and the First World War.* Cambridge: Cambridge University Press.

Curran, James. 1978. The Press as an Agency of Social Control: An Historical Perspective. In George Boyce, James Curran and Pauline Wingate (eds), *Newspaper History from the Seventeenth Century to the Present Day.* London: Constable.

Dandeker, Christopher. 1990. *Surveillance, Power and Modernity.* Cambridge: Polity.

Dawson, Graham. 1994. *Soldier Heroes: British Adventure, Empire and the Imagining of Masculinities.* London: Routledge.

De Marly, Diana. 1986. *Working Dress: A History of Occupational Clothing.* London: Batsford Books.

Edwards, Elizabeth. 2001. *Raw Histories: Photographs, Anthropology and Museums.* Oxford: Berg.

Farrar, Martin. 1998. *News from the Front: War Correspondents on the Western Front 1914–18.* Stroud: Sutton Publishing.

Foucault, Michel. 1991. *Discipline and Punish: The Birth of the Prison.* London: Penguin.

Fuller, Captain J. F. C. 1911. *Hints on Training Territorial Infantry from Recruit to Trained Soldier.* London: Gale & Polden.

Fuller, Captain J. F. C. 1914. *Training Soldiers for War.* London: Hugh Rees.

Fussell, Paul. 1975. *The Great War and Modern Memory.* Oxford: Oxford University Press.

Giedion, Siegfried. 1948. *Mechanization Takes Command: A Contribution to Anonymous History.* New York: Oxford University Press.

Gilbert, Martin. 1995. *First World War.* London: HarperCollins.

Gregory, Adrian. 2004. A Clash of Cultures: The British Press and the Opening of the Great War. In Troy R. E. Paddock (ed.), *A Call to Arms: Propaganda, Public Opinion and Newspapers in the Great War.* Westport: Praeger.

Hamilton, General Ian. 1913. *National Life and National Training.* London: P. S. King.

Hindess, Barry. 1996. *Discourses of Power: From Hobbes to Foucault.* Oxford: Blackwell.

Horrall, Andrew. 2001. *Popular Culture in London c.1890–1918.* Manchester: Manchester University Press.

Hynes, Samuel. 1990. *A War Imagined: The First World War and English Culture.* London: Bodley Head.

Kern, Stephen. 1983. *The Culture of Time and Space 1889–1918.* London: Weidenfeld & Nicolson.

Kipling, Rudyard. 1915. *The New Army in Training.* London: Macmillan.

Kracauer, Siegfried. 1995. *The Mass Ornament: Weimar Essays.* Cambridge, MA: Harvard University Press.

Lewinski, Jorge. 1978. *The Camera at War.* London: W. H. Allen.

Lovelace, Colin. 1978. British press censorship during the First World War. In George Boyce, James Curran and Pauline Wingate (eds), *Newspaper History from the Seventeenth Century to the Present Day.* London: Constable.

Low, Rachel. 1973. *The History of the British Film 1914–18.* London: Allen & Unwin.

Lyon, David. 1994. *The Electronic Eye: The Rise of Surveillance Society.* Minneapolis: University of Minnesota Press.

MacKenzie, J. M. 1984. *Propaganda and Empire: The Manipulation of British Public Opinion 1880–1960.* Manchester: Manchester University Press.

Marquis, Alice G. 1978. Words as Weapons: Propaganda in Britain and Germany During the First World War. *Journal of Contemporary History* 13: 467–98.

Martin, Michèle. 2006. *Images at War: Illustrated Periodicals and Constructed Nations.* Toronto: University of Toronto Press.

McEwan, J. M. 1982. The National Press during the First World War: Ownership and Circulation. *Journal of Contemporary History* 17: 459–86.

Morgan, David H. J. 1994. Theater of War: Combat, the Military and Masculinities. In Harry Brod and Michael Kaufman (eds) *Theorizing Masculinities.* London: Sage, pp. 165–182.

Moriarty, Catherine. 2003. Through a Picture Only: Photography and Commemoration. In Gail Braybon, *Evidence, History and the Great War: Historians and the Impact of 1914–18.* Oxford: Berghahn Books.

Myerly, Scott Hughes. 1996. *British Military Spectacle: From the Napoleonic Wars through the Crimea* Cambridge: Harvard University Press.

Paris, Michael. 2000. *Warrior Nation: Images of War in British Popular Culture 1850–2000.* London: Reaktion Books.

Pick, Daniel. 1993. *War Machine: The Rationalisation of Slaughter in the Modern Age.* New Haven, CT and London: Yale University Press.

Rabinbach, Anson. 1990. *The Human Motor: Energy, Fatigue, and the Origins of Modernity.* Berkeley, CA: University of California Press.

Rawson, Andrew. 2006. *British Army Handbook 1914–1918.* Stroud: Sutton Publishing.

Rimmer, Edmund. 1917. *The Story of The First-Fifth Bedfords.* Manchester: Co-operative Wholesale Society's Printing Works.

Searle, G.R. 2003. The Politics of National Efficiency and of War, 1900–1918. In Chris Wigley (ed.), *A Companion to Early Twentieth Century Britain.* Oxford: Blackwell.

Sekula, Allan. 1986. The Body and the Archive. *October* 39 (Winter): 3–64.

Sekula, Allan. 1999. Reading an archive: photography between labour and capital. In Jessica Evans and Stuart Hall, *Visual Culture: The Reader.* London: Sage.

Shaw, Martin. 1984 (ed.), *War, State and Society.* London: Macmillan.

Silbey, David. 2005. *The British Working Class and Enthusiasm for War, 1914–1916.* London: Frank Cass.

Solano, Captain E. John. 1915. *Drill and Field Training* [Imperial Army Series]. London: John Murray.

Stewart, Ian and Carruthers, Susan. 1996. *War, Culture and the Media: Representations of the Military in Twentieth Century Britain.* London: Flicks Books.

Synott, Anthony. 1993. *The Body Social: Symbolism, Self and Society.* London: Routledge.

Tagg, John. 1988. *The Burden of Representation: Essays on Photographies and Histories.* Basingstoke: Palgrave Macmillan.

Tate, Trudi. 1998. *Modernism, History and the First World War.* Manchester: Manchester University Press.

Taylor, A. J. P. 2005. *War by Time-Table: How the First World War Began.* London: Leo Cooper.

Tickner, Lisa. 2000. *Modern Life and Modern Subjects.* London: New Haven.

Ugolini, Laura. 2007. *Men and Menswear: Sartorial Consumption in Britain 1880–1939* Aldershot: Ashgate.

War Office. 1914. *Infantry Training.* London: HMSO.

Warner Merien, Mary. 2006. *Photography: A Cultural History.* London: Laurence King.

Williams, Raymond. 1978. The Press and Popular Culture: An Historical Perspective. In George Boyce, James Curran and Pauline Wingate (eds), *Newspaper History from the Seventeenth Century to the Present Day.* London: Constable.

Winter Jay M. 1995. British National Identity and the First World War. In S. J. Green and R. C. Whiting (eds), *The Boundaries of the State in Modern Britain.* Cambridge: Cambridge University Press.

Winter, Jay M. 1985. *The Great War and The British People.* London: Macmillan.

Winter, Jay M. 1999. Popular Culture in Wartime Britain. In Aviel Roshwald and Richard Stites, *European Culture in the Great War.* Cambridge: Cambridge University Press.

Wombell, Paul. 1986. Face to Face with Themselves: Photography and the First World War. In Patricia Holland, Jo Spence and Simon Watney (eds), *Photography/Politics: Two.* London: Comedia.

**Photography
& Culture**

Volume 2—Issue 2
July 2009
pp. 153–170
DOI:
10.2752/175145109X12456654102768

Performing the Relational Archive

Merav Yerushalmy

Merav Yerushalmy is currently conducting her postdoctoral research at the University of Haifa in Israel, focusing on issues of communality, documentation, and social and political engagement in contemporary Israeli art. In her doctoral research, she addressed the changes in photographic theory and practice in recent years, as well as the developments in relational and participatory discourse, continuing her long-standing interests developed when working in community galleries and socially engaged art projects.

Abstract

This article addresses the recent changes in archival practices and discourse, and their implications for documentary photography and photographic theory. Exploring the work of artists such as Renée Green and Gitte Villesen, as well as the writings of Margaret Iversen, Jan Verwoert, and others, the first section of the article examines the severing of the links between photographic images and the events they document in the photographic theory of the late 1970s and 1980s, and the rethinking of these links today through the concepts of performativity and relationality. The second half of the article examines more closely the discourse of the archive in the last decade, focusing on the work of Benjamin Buchloh and Hal Foster. The article highlights the shifts in recent archival practices, from an excavation of past events and their traumatic implications, to viewing of the archive as a potential site for (re)constructing utopian visions.

Keywords: archive, relationality, documentary photography, photography theory, performative

Introduction

In an article published a couple of years ago in *Art Monthly*, the critic Sarah James addressed the development of photographic theory and practice in the last decade. She wrote:

> Photographic art practices have continued to proliferate in the last decade, yet we have not witnessed an analogously rich growth in photographic theory. No new paradigm of thinking about photography has emerged... Photography has long been accepted into the cannon of art, legitimised by a substantial body of poststructuralist theories. However, in today's art world, defined for some by relational aesthetics and a biennale art of social participation, process, collaboration and installation, photography occupies a privileged autonomous place within both museum and market, like that enjoyed by artworks that were once the subject of photography's critique. (James 2006: 8)

The need to rethink photographic theory and contextualize it within contemporary socially engaged practices arises, for James, out of what she sees as the waning ability of poststructuralist theories to provide a productive critical framework for photographic practice.

"Several issues must be addressed in any elaboration of contemporary photographic art practices," says James. These issues include the "complete lack of any significant development in photographic theory in the last decade; the continued analysis of the medium in 'outmoded' semiotic or ideological terms; the need to focus upon the implications of postmodern theories upon photography instead of understanding photography to be a symptom of postmodernism; the institutional politics surrounding photography in the present art world, and the unsatisfactorily

analysed position held by documentary and the documentary aesthetic." In regard to documentary photography, it is especially the "long neglected categories of truth, history and agency" which have often been bracketed by the poststructuralist discourse and which James finds in urgent need of reappraisal (James 2006: 8).

James' timely analysis of photographic theory and her call to explore its development in the last decade (and possibly in the previous two decades as well), might provide a cursory outline of a discursive space which borders on socially engaged art on the one hand, and photographic theory on the other, and seeks to understand and perhaps resolve some of the impasses of photographic theory today. The juxtaposition of social (as well as political) issues and photography has been a recurrent theme since the emergence of photographic documentation in the nineteenth century. The main thrust of James' arguments however, lies in the specific theoretical and historical contexts in which she positions these issues, calling for a rethinking of photography theory at a time when the impact of poststructuralism and its close affiliation with photography might begin to be reassessed.

The aim of this article is twofold. It wishes to contribute to the discourse of photographic theory, highlighting aspects of its recent history as well as contemporary practices, but also to address today's socially engaged art, and explore the roles photography plays within it.

Coming to prominence in the last two decades, socially engaged art, also referred to as participatory art, discursive site specificity, relational aesthetics, and dialogical art to name but a few of the terms commonly used, is a loose affiliation of practices and discourses which are often based in relational or communal approaches to art making and viewing. Grounded in institutional critique, conceptual practices, public art, and political activism, socially engaged art has been associated in the last years with writers and curators such as Miwon Kwon, Grant Kester, Claire Bishop, Maria Lind, Nicholas Bourriaud, and others, and with a wide range of artists—from Rirkrit Tiravanija and Liam Gillick to Renée Green, Francis Alÿs, and Jeremy Deller, to name but a few. Today's socially engaged art has developed at a time in which the number of international art exhibitions and biennales has risen significantly, and has, in some respects, come to typify these events, in which curators and organizers vie for "local" and site-specific works of art such as those provided by the contingent and participatory socially engaged art.

Seen from within the field of socially engaged art, photography seems, at least initially, to have a very limited role, as socially engaged practices are most often grounded in performance, installation, and site-specific work rather than photography or other forms of documentation. Observed more carefully however, it becomes clear that the documentation of socially engaged performances and installations, as well as the use of documentary photography itself as a relational form, is much more extensive than one may assume. Almost all artists practicing socially engaged art in its many and varied forms, use some sort of documentation, and for many of them, such as Renée Green discussed in this article, documentation (photographic and other) not only serves

to record social interaction, but also to facilitate it. It is somewhat surprising then, that the theoretical discourse of socially engaged art has devoted very few texts exclusively to these issues so far, and even more rarely considered them within the context of photography theory.[1] In a parallel move, photography theory itself has also mostly ignored the developments in socially engaged practices of recent years, and thus a valuable research course has been left largely unexplored. One site, in which the relations between social engagement and practices of documentation have been addressed however, is that of the archive. Employing various documentary modes, as well as facilitating and performing various interpersonal, communal, and historical relations, the site of the archive might provide us with some insights missing in the fields of both socially engaged art and photography theory.

Performative and Relational Documentation at the Site of the Archive

One of the most interesting texts published in recent years on the performative, and I would argue, also socially engaged archive has been written by Jan Verwoert and is the introduction to *Untitled (Experience of Place)*—a collection of essays written by critics and artists such as Michael Ashkin, Matthew Buckingham, and Tacita Dean (Verwoert 2003: 9–23). In his introduction, Verwoert traces the changes in the practices of documentation and archiving in the last decades—from the deconstruction of the universal archive in the 1990s to the participatory archival projects of today.

Verwoert begins by looking at artworks that expose the fragility and temporality of the once potent archive. Christian Boltanski's *Jewish School of Grosse Hamburgerstrasse in Berlin in 1938* (1994)—a series of black and white photographs enlarged from the original images of a class of Jewish children in Berlin in 1938—serves for Verwoert as a potent example. In the work, the vulnerability of the images which indicate imminent loss, not less (if not more), than they point to the preservation of memory, demonstrate both the impossibility of the archival mission, and our lingering desire to sustain it. Verwoert acknowledges the importance of works such as Boltanski's, which he says "discourage the fantasy that universal mastery of history as a totality [is] possible, [by] invoking the ideas of universality and totality only to frustrate the viewer by placing them beyond her grasp" (Verwoert 2003: 11). By presenting the archive in an almost untempered, straightforward manner, says Verwoert, Boltanski manages to arouse our desire for mastery over the image, and demonstrate the futility and precariousness of this desire at the same time.

This move, which sets out to highlight our fantasy of complete mastery, continues Verwoert, however important and productive, has its limitations however. For "once this point [regarding the vulnerability of the archive] is made, it can only be reiterated," and thus, while "you can certainly refresh the sublime experience of inadequacy in relation to history by gazing into the abyss from time to time … where does that take you in the long run?" (Verwoert 2003: 11). Thus, what had been a valuable practice, opening up new avenues of discussions regarding the documentary image, memory,

and the archive, had thus run its course, and left the field open for new conceptualizations of the documentary and the archive.

One such conceptualization, according to Verwoert, has emerged in the form of the personal and therefore necessarily partial archive. Whereas Boltanski's work focused on demonstrating the inadequacy of the universal archive, a new generation of artists has begun to rummage through the archive's ruins, and explore the critical potency of what has been left to them. Instead of reiterating the fragmentary, local, and subjective nature of the document as an alternative to the previous universal concepts of the archive, this new generation of artists, including (amongst others) Mark Dion, Fred Wilson, Tacita Dean, and Renée Green, uses the partial archive to construct purposely incomplete but nonetheless potent historical narratives.

In Green's work especially, the critical power of the partial archive, not only in deconstructing essentialized historical or cultural representations, but also in presenting, analyzing, and constructing alternative histories based on partial and personal encounters, has been paramount. Like Dion, Wilson, and other artists, Green often uses documentary photography, video documentation, objects, and texts to construct "research rooms" in which audiences may engage with the material on hand, as well as with each other. In *Import/ Export Funk Office*, for example, exhibited in Cologne and other places from 1992 onwards, Green installed a "research room" dedicated to American hip-hop music and its reception in Germany.[2] For this work, Green had researched several cases pertaining to German-African American cultural relations, one of which focused on the relationship between the German philosopher Theodor Adorno and the American activist Angela Davis. Davis, who had studied with Adorno in Frankfurt, returned to the United States in the mid-1960s where she played a major role in the Black Panthers. Green's work had ultimately taken on its current form through a chance encounter with Diederich Diederichsen—a German music critic with whom she had stayed in Cologne during the preparations for the exhibition. It was only then, that she discovered the crucial impact of black hip-hop on the German music scene, and Diederichsen's significant role in introducing hip-hop to Germany, and decided to focus on these relations. The installation itself, as it was exhibited in 1997

in the Chicago Museum of Contemporary Art, was an office like space, which included metal shelves filled with books, cassettes and videotapes, as well as four desks that served as "funk stations," and photographs of Green's New York and Diederichsen's Cologne apartments. Green supplied white gloves and magnifying glasses, enabling viewers to study the pictures and music collections in detail. She also provided boom boxes for listening to music, speeches, and interviews, and displayed Diederichsen's entire collection of records and CDs. Texts on the walls translated terms such as "rap" and "hood" into German, and contributed, along with the gloves and magnifying glass, to the archival/research function and feel of the installation.[3]

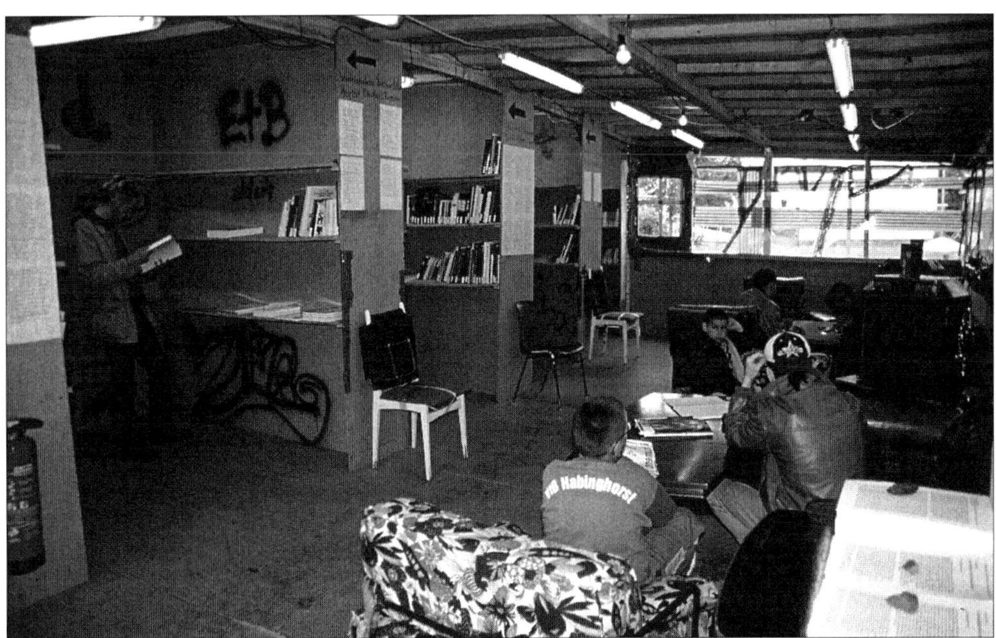

Fig 1 Thomas Hirschhorn, *Bataille Monument*, 2002 (Bibliothek) "Documenta 11," Kassel, 2002 (photo: Werner Maschmann), courtesy Gladstone Gallery, New York.

Photography & Culture   Volume 2—Issue 2—July 2009, pp. 153–170

Other research projects, such as Thomas Hirschhorn's *Bataille Monument* created for the 11th Kassel Documenta in 2002 (Figure 1), have also utilized and facilitated cultural and communal relations. In his work, part of the Monuments series, Hirschhorn collaborated with the Turkish-German residents of a local housing estate in Kassel, designing and building a series of precarious structures, which included (amongst others), a library of books relating to Georges Bataille, an exhibition featuring a three-dimensional map of Bataille's work, a television studio, a stand with food and drinks, and a shuttle service taking residents and visitors to and from the Documenta exhibitions located in the city center. Like Green's investigation and performance of German-African American relations, Hirschhorn's project also provided a research space in which numerous documents, photographic and other, were made available to the audience who could use them in a variety of ways. Despite employing relatively similar practices, and addressing very similar issues regarding cultural relations, Green and Hirschhorn's works provide two very different approaches to the issues at hand.

The most crucial difference between the works lies in the nature of the cultural relations facilitated and portrayed by them. For while Green's work emphasized the reciprocity of the cultural practices of African-Americans and Germans and highlighted their shared critical ambitions, Hirschhorn's work had been declared by the artist himself, as not being about social or cultural relations at all. In a charged statement often repeated by critics referring to the work, Hirschhorn claimed that "I am not a social worker," and elsewhere that his works are "work[s] of art, and not socio-cultural project[s]."[4] Despite Hirschhorn's claims and their (often less than critical) reception, the participation of the estate residents in the construction and running of the work and the actual presence of the work within the estate's premises, were of major importance to the artist himself, the audiences, the residents, and the art world at large. These relations were quite complex and multilayered. They included paternalism (Hirschhorn notes in one of his lectures how "keen and interested" in Bataille's work the residents had been), genuine and amicable conviviality from both sides, potential exploitation (the residents were only paid minimal wages for their work on the installation), and violence (the works were vandalized during their installment) (Hirschhorn 2003). These relations also aroused some heated theoretical debate. Maria Lind, a Swedish curator who has been involved in various socially engaged art projects in recent years, compared Hirschhorn's work to that of the Turkish group Oda Projesi. She wrote:

> The residents in the working class neighbourhood [in which Hirschhorn installed his work] appeared as a different and colourful element in a project that was primarily a criticism of an art genre and not of social structures. Hirschhorn's work has therefore understandably been criticised for "exhibiting" and making exotic marginalised groups and thereby contributing to a form of a social pornography. Thomas Hirschhorn himself wanted to test what is possible within the framework of the world's most prestigious contemporary art exhibition. Whereas

[he] makes a distinction between social projects and art projects—his own work clearly belonging to the second category—such a distinction is more difficult to make for Oda Projesi. They have loose connections with the art world and are less occupied with discussing what is and is not art; it seems to suffice that art offers a method and a zone for certain types of activities. At the same time, they work with groups of people in their immediate environments and allow them to wield great influence on the project. Therefore, Oda Projesi's work is both social and artistic, but without an official commissioner—for instance, a local authority—that expects social reform or measurable improvements. (Lind 2004)

Lind's distinction between artworks which are "both social and artistic" and those that define themselves exclusively in artistic terms was taken up by Claire Bishop in a recent paper published in *Artforum* and titled "The Social Turn: Collaboration and Its Discontents" (Bishop 2006: 178–84). Unlike Lind who sees the conflation of the social and the aesthetic as a positive development in the work of such artists and groups as the Oda Projesi, Bishop attributes more merit to works thay are firmly located within the discourse and practice of art. Thus, while Lind can easily understand why Hirschhorn's work had been criticized as a form of social exploitation, Bishop claims that such criticism sidelines "the conceptual density and artistic significance of artworks in favour of an appraisal of the artists' relationship with their collaborators," and replaces aesthetic considerations with ethical ones (Bishop 2006: 180).

Comparing Hirschhorn's work with that of Green may help to clarify some of the issues raised in the debates about his works, as well as other socially engaged practices. According to Lind, part of the difficulty with works such as Hirschhorn's lies with the fact that the work is predetermined by the author, and is hardly impacted by the collaborators' input—assigning them the role of mere assistants and executors rather than co-authorship. In the *Bataille Monument,* the estate residents served as day laborers, taxi drivers, cafeteria workers, and local guides, and had very little influence over the work's concept and its philosophical contents. But compared with Hirschhorn's *Bataille Monument,* Green's projects (in their conceptualization and installation stages) are even less participatory, as Green usually works with a few chosen individuals in the initial stages of the work, and only opens it out to participants after its installation. But whereas Hirschhorn's work can be read as both exposing but also reiterating existing power relations—reinforcing stereotypical roles in which the artist is cast as the protagonist of philosophical knowledge and the estate residents as menial service providers, in Green's work, the audience, artist, and the various cultural groups are all presented as potential partners. This partnership does not necessarily imply equal socioeconomic and cultural opportunities, nor is it based in a utopian social vision in which all power struggles have been resolved, but it does presume a shared critical ambition that is not exclusively based in cultural identity. Thus, unlike Hirschhorn's critical approach in which existing disparities are (at least partially) reaffirmed, Green's critical approach is grounded in the exploration of the critical practices exhibited by practitioners of various cultural identities.

The critical role of the audience in her artworks is described by Green using the term "participatory mobility" (Green 1999: 3). By this term, she refers to the active investment of the viewers/participators in piecing together the different and often highly complex parts of her artworks. In a manner parallel to that played by the sublime in Boltanski's works, Green's amassment of texts, photographs, and other archival objects, as well as the active effort required to sift through the vast amount of information provided, is designed to challenge and frustrate the desire to master the work. Rather than a heightened sense of precariousness and a void however, Green's work attempts to undermine the desire for mastery by creating a baffling and over-determined "puzzle" of meanings. This strategy is a recurring one in Green's art. In *Partially Buried in Three Parts*, for example, first shown at Pat Hearn's Gallery in New York in 1996, Green created a multilayered work exploring issues of identity and historical memory, which span three decades and three continents. The work addressed Robert's Smithson *Partially Buried Shed* installed in Ohio's Kent State University in 1970 (where Green's mother was a student), and the shooting of four students at the May 4th rally at the university. Its second part explored the representation of 1970s America both in Germany and locally as seen by Americans of German descent. In the work's third and final part, Green exhibited photographs of Korea, where the work had been originally installed in its three-part form. These included images from the Korean War and from modern-day Korea

that Green took herself, and referred, once again, to issues of American international relations. As in her *Import/Export Funk Office*, the audiences were required to invest a substantial effort in order to piece together the various parts of the work—a task which could not be easily or fully accomplished, not only because of the mass of information present, but also because of the intricate and idiosyncratic relations between the work's various aspects.

Green's archival installations assign the document (whether photographic, textual or in video form) some of the roles traditionally assigned to reportage, most basic of which is the taking of an active interest in the world beyond the document's own representational strategies. However, unlike traditional reportage, Green's documents do not assert the "world beyond" or essentialize its nature, nor do they disregard the crucial role representational strategies have in determining our perception of the world "out there." Rather, through the performance of their own open-ended, over-determined nature as documentary texts/images, Green's idiosyncratic archives manage to question the relations between events in the world beyond, as well as their own existence as documentary representations.

The performative aspects of photographic documents and their relations to the world beyond the image itself have been recently taken up in several theoretical works. In one such essay, titled *Following Pieces: On Performative Photography*, Margaret Iversen writes on what she defines as the "performative realism" of photographic practice (Iversen 2006: 91–109). By this term, she refers to an ongoing interest in the documentation of "reality," stretching from André Breton to Gabriel Orozco, a documentation that does not seek to record a transparent image of an event, nor to retrieve and revive its traces, but rather to follow and discover it as it unfolds. Iversen writes:

> The photo-document as performative realism does not record some pre-existing object or state of affairs. Rather, the camera is treated like an instrument of discovery, such as a telescope... Photography imagined in these terms would have a very different nature from Barthes' conjuring of the uncanny photographic "return of the dead" in *Camera Lucida*. Barthes' photograph revives the image of a lost object; what I will call performative photography tracks and records a contemporary event. Like the narrative of [André Breton's] *Nadja*, such photography *follows* the event, not knowing the conclusion in advance. (Iversen 2006: 93–4)

Iversen's understanding of the relations between the event and its documentation in terms of *following and discovery* rather than a recording of preexisting events is highly interesting, and could be quite productive in considering the documentation of socially engaged art. For conceptualizing the camera as a telescope, or perhaps more accurately as a periscope focused on the discovery of the world "out there" as its events unfolds, would allow us to think of the photographic act, not as reviving or mourning a past event, nor as actively constructing its own imagery, but rather as being curious and attentive towards the world outside it—an approach which the documentation of socially engaged art often takes.

Iversen's understanding of photography's performative realism is interesting not only in the genealogy of performative photography it elaborates, beginning with Breton, continuing with Vito Acconci and Sophie Calle, and concluding with Gabriel Orozco, but also in the discursive context it provides for these practices. In the passage quoted above, Iversen already mentions the differences she sees between the ongoing engagement of performative photography with the event, and Roland Barthes' approach in which photography serves to facilitate the "uncanny return of the dead" by "reviving the image of a lost object."[5] For Iversen, performative photography may be seen as an alternative to Barthes' understanding of the photographic act, as it is the ongoing event, rather than the past one, that is the crux of her reading of performative photographic practices.

Iversen's concept of the performative photo-document however, does not only provide an alternative to Barthes' understanding of photography, but it may also present a challenge to other readings of photography, especially those offered by poststructuralist and postmodernist theories. With its emphasis on the recording of the unfolding event, Iversen's approach brings into play once again, the role of photography as documenting a world "out there." Compared with postmodernist approaches, such as those advocated by Douglas Crimp, in which photography was often seen as essentially a self-referential medium divorced from (rather than curious towards) events outside itself, Iversen's approach presents a rather striking alternative. Going back to one of Crimp's most influential accounts of photography, *The Photographic Activity of Postmodernism*, one is struck by Crimp's vigorous reading of the photograph as a poststructuralist edifice that shuns almost all references to events outside itself (Crimp 1980: 91–101).[6] In the essay, which was based on works by Sherrie Levine, Cindy Sherman, and Richard Prince, and was reworked from a previous version published in Crimp's *Pictures* catalog, photographic activity is described as referring almost exclusively to other images and the act of photographing itself, rather than the world beyond. Crimp's approach, which soon became *the* photographic strategy of choice for many contemporary artists and writers, claimed that photography was essentially the "representation of the always-already-seen," and that rather than searching for the original and authentic, it is the "purloined, confiscated, appropriated [and] stolen" image that photography is best suited to deploy (Crimp 1995: 118). Although Crimp's very useful and timely deconstruction of the ideas of the original, the authentic, and the self had indeed opened up new ways to reconsider the (re)presentational nature of photography and its embeddedness in a web of existing imagery, the strong emphasis that he and later others put on these approaches had almost obliterated all considerations of the relations between the image and the events outside it. As Sarah James, quoted in the introduction, claims, the unqualified employment of postmodernist theories in regard to photographic materials has resulted in curtailing the ability of photographic discourse to address the crucial issues of truth, agency, and history in photographic practices today.

In the context of Iversen's reading of photography as a performative practice, it is interesting to note the sharp distinction Crimp draws between practices of performance and photography. Contrasting the "eventness" of the performance, for which, he writes, you "literally had to be there," with the noted absence of the event in photography, he claims that it is this very absence of the event that is the essential "condition of representation" of photographic practice (Crimp 1995: 109). Photography's discourse, he says, would benefit from acknowledging this absence of the event, and rather than attempting to capture the event as accurately as possible, should turn its attention away from it and towards the investigation of its own representational modes.

Compared with Crimp's sharp distinction between the performativity of the event and the eventless absence of the photograph, Iversen's concept of "performative realism" offers a "rehabilitation" of the severed ties between the event and its photographic documentation. Although Iversen does not attempt to reconstruct the "true" and "authentic" image of reality that Crimp deconstructed so well, she does attempt to rethink the relations between notions of the world "out there"—however mediated, fluctuating, and partial our perceptions of it may be, and the photographic accounts of it, positing them once again as operating, if not together, than at least side by side.

The relations between the event and its documentation, which Iversen's essay conjures and Douglas Crimp's text severs, have also been addressed by Peggy Phelan. In her account of the ontology of performance, Phelan sets out her view of the relations between performance and its documentation, a view that is not so different from that of Crimp. She writes:

> Performance's only life is in the present, it cannot be saved, recorded, documented or otherwise participate in the circulation of representations of representations *of* representations: once it does so, it becomes something other than performance. To the degree that performance enters the economy of reproduction it betrays and lessens the promise of its own ontology. Performance's being, like the ontology of subjectivity proposed here, becomes itself through disappearance. (Phelan 1993: 146)

Thus, like Crimp, Phelan distinguishes between the event, for which you had to be there, and its reproduction (photographic or other), which only manages to destroy the event's precarious existence. Unlike Crimp, however, and despite her conceptualization of performance as existing outside the "economy of reproduction," Phelan does see a possibility of documenting and writing about performance and performative events (a practice in which she is heavily invested in). Discussing this possibility, she says:

> To attempt to write about the undocumentable event of performance is to invoke the rules of the written document and thereby alter the event itself. Just as quantum physics discovered that macro-instruments cannot measure microscopic particles without transforming those particles, so too must performance critics realize that the labor to write about performance (and thus to preserve it) is also a labor that fundamentally alters the event. It does no good, however, to simply refuse to write about performance because of this inescapable transformation. The challenge raised by the ontological claims of performance for writing is to re-mark again the performative possibilities of writing itself. The act of writing towards disappearance, rather than the act of writing towards preservation, must remember that the after-effect of disappearance is the experience of subjectivity itself. (Phelan 1993: 148)

The documenting of the event according to Phelan, does not necessarily follow the event itself (except in a chronological manner), but rather rediscovers its own performative nature, while transforming the nature of the "original" event. The idea of documentation as a transformative practice which Phelan so eloquently describes, is not so far removed from that of Iversen's "performative realism" (and indeed Iversen refers to Phelan in her essay), but it does provide a rather subtle and potentially meaningful shift of emphasis. For, although the documentary act in both Iversen and Phelan's accounts is described as an autonomous practice—one which is not simply caused by the event itself but has a life of its own—in Peggy Phelan's work this autonomy is more pronounced, while in Iversen's text, the documentary act, even if not subordinate to the event, continues to follow it physically as well as conceptually. Thus, while for Phelan the documentary act is an essentially creative one, focused on discovering its own performativity through its re-creation of the past event, in Iversen's essay the documentary continues to perform the work of the periscope, focusing on the discovery of the ongoing event, rather than on its creation or transformation.

The distinction between Iversen and Phelan's notions of performative photography can be elaborated further, when comparing Renée Green's approach to the documentation of her own works, to that taken by Gitte Villesen—a Danish artist whose works have been discussed within the context of relational aesthetics.[7]

In 1993, Green began to consider the documentation of her own works more seriously. In a book titled *Certain Miscellanies—Some Documents* published by De Appel Foundation in 1996, Green reflects on the transformation of the *Import/ Export Funk Office* piece into a digital format (Van Duyn 1996: 70–92).[8] Although the technological advancements and especially the rising prominence of the World Wide Web have rendered some of Green's considerations obsolete, her writing still provides useful insights into the theoretical considerations involved in her documentary work. She writes:

> Since the work "import export funk office" in part refers to the process of information gathering and international, national and local transfer of cultural products (specifically hip hop music and various material produced as a result of the African diaspora in this case, although it alludes to other forms of cultural commerce as well) it lent itself very well to a digital transformation which makes the information which was gathered accessible, but in a playful and hopefully compelling form which links sound, text, video, photos, magazines and books. Thus the disk is a new work. (Van Duyn 1996: 71)

Green's description of the CD in relation to the initial event, in this case the physical installation of the work, provides an almost too neat an example of what Phelan describes. Green, like Phelan, conceives of the documentation or "writing" of the original event as a new performative piece, one that not only reorders but also transforms the past event in the process of its "writing." Rather than "capturing" or reiterating the installation in a straightforward, direct manner, Green re-created it so as to enable a performative exploration of the data amassed for the original installation in a new form. This form was not only new in its handling and exposition of the material, but also emphasized, due to its mobile and easily distributed nature, some issues regarding the dissemination of cultural products in a globalized market that had been less prominent in the original installation. Thus, as Phelan anticipates, Green's "original" work would over time be "written into disappearance," and supplemented or replaced by a digital version that simultaneously draws on it and departs from it.

Like Green's work, Gitte Villesen's art is highly performative, and explores various practices of documentation; and like Green, Villesen employs the personal and the partial archive in her work, as well as many "found documents"—from the single record to entire collections. In *Willy as DJ* (1995) for example, Villesen uses video to document the record collection of the work's main protagonist—Willy. Monologues, dialogues, playing records, singing, recounting of personal and cultural history, and even dancing with Villesen herself are all employed in the performance of Willy's musical archive, and present a rich and nuanced usage of both the collection and its documentation. Unlike Green's works however, Villesen's video art does not present us with an installation available for browsing, but with a specific performance of an archive, one which can be interpreted in various ways, but which does not provide an immediate access to the documents themselves. Compared with Green's works, Villesen's archives are also much less dense, both conceptually and in terms of the sheer quantity of material amassed, and are thus much easier to navigate. Yet despite their relatively simple and more mediated structure, the interest of Villesen's works lie in the nature of their approach to documentation. For unlike Green's documented events, which have usually occurred in the past and are "brought back to life" through their re-inscription in the archive, Villesen's events are continuous and their documentation is an ongoing act whose outcome is unknown. Like Iversen's model of performative photography, in which the camera serves as a periscope—an instrument for discovering and following events, Villesen's camera is also employed as a "tentacle" for sensing and documenting ongoing happenings as they occur.

Like some of the conceptual artists Iversen describes, Villesen is involved not only in the documentation of events, but in their performance as well, and combines in these performances both conceptual, task-setting elements as well as more open-ended and personal ones. Describing Sophie's Calle's *Suite Vénitienne* (1980), in which the artist followed and documented an individual (Henri B) in Venice, Iversen writes on the confluence of these two aspects in performative photography:

Calle's project is aptly described as performative photography because, on the one hand, there are the elements of task-setting, of submitting herself to arbitrary structures and the consequent authorial divestiture. One the other hand, there is the re-orientation of the picture toward the recording of an ongoing, open-ended event open to unanticipated consequences. (Iversen 2006: 102)

The setting of a task defined by simple and non-affective means, such as following an individual and recording the ensuing events, combined with a specifically oriented act instigated by the artist herself, allows Calle to produce a work in which the photograph does not seek to capture a reality "out there," but records an event that was indeterminately yet personally set off by her. In a similar manner, Villesen's work could also be described as performing a "task," one in which she does not follow others from afar, but interacts with them. As in Calle's works, it is Villesen's own decisions that set off the events, and despite her actual participation in them (such as dancing with Willy), Villesen does not control the ensuing occurrences but remains curious towards them and slightly aloof. Like Calle, Villesen's initial tasks, such as meeting a collector of music or lace, or interacting with someone in a summer fete (which can be seen in some of her other works), seem simple, but as in Calle's works, these initial tasks set in motion events that often carry significant emotional weight and provide us with personal, relational, and even historical insights. This "conceptual relationality," which Villesen's work develops—an interpersonal "procedure" initiated by a simple imperative and developed for its "own sake" (rather than the procuring of a direct and "authentic" knowledge of the other), allows Villesen to extend the concept of performative photography as described by Iversen, and employ it in the highly charged practices of documenting others. Veering away from direct voyeurism (although some aspects of it, such as the fascination by, and desiring of others do remain), Villesen's performative photography maintains a curious and attentive approach towards the ongoing events she sets off, yet avoids constituting the works' subjects as grounded in a fixed and essentialized identity. Thus, like Green, Villesen offers a new model of documentation, one that neither recoils into investigating only its own means of representation, nor attempts to "capture" the "authentic" other, but experiments with new ways of engaging with the world "out there" and its subjects.

Reconsidering the Archive

The changes in the practices and discourse of the archive, and the growing interest in the relational and socially engaged aspects of documentation are made evident when examining two significant essays on the archive published in the last decade. The first, written by Benjamin Buchloh on the archival work of Gerhard Richter, and titled "Gerhard Richter's Atlas: The Anomic Archive" was published in 1999, while the second, written by Hal Foster on contemporary archival practices and titled "An Archival Impulse" was published five years later in 2004 (Buchloh 2000; Foster 2004).

Buchloh begins his exploration of Richter's work, by briefly referring to the archival works of Christian Boltanski and

Bernd and Hilla Becher. As is the case with Richter's Atlas, says Buchloh, the wide scope and complex discursive orders of these projects have not been adequately addressed by the existing discourse, and it is the aim of his essay to offer some much needed theoretical frameworks in which to situate such archival works.[9] Although archival practices have received more attention since 1999 when Buchloh originally published his essay, the usage and functioning of archives in contemporary art, as well as the various modes of documentation which they employ have, as Sarah James suggests, remained relatively under-researched in today's discourse.

Referring to the first twelve panels of Richter's Atlas, Buchloh discusses the lack of conceptual frameworks in which to contextualize Richter's work. He writes that "Despite the first impression that the Atlas might provide, neither the private album of the amateur, nor the cumulative projects of documentary photography could identify the discursive order of this photographic collection" (Buchloh 2000: 12). Buchloh also discounts topographical photography, surveillance practices, advertising, and photojournalism as potential frameworks for deciphering Richter's Atlas, as these only allow for a partial understanding of the work and are relevant to specific images rather than the project as a whole. Reading the first twelve panels of the Atlas, Buchloh charts the work's progression, which begins with Richter's familial snapshots, and moves on to more banal, pop and consumerist images. The first "chapter" of the Atlas ends, says Buchloh, with images of Jewish captives in the Nazi concentration camps, which are the first historical images included in the work. It is then, with the images of the captives, writes Buchloh, that there is a "sudden revelation: that there is still one link that binds an image to its referent within the apparently empty barrage of photographic imagery and the universal production of sign exchange value: the trauma from which the compulsion to repress originated" (Buchloh 2000: 30). Thus, it is the trauma that serves to link the otherwise vacant photographic images to the "world at large"—a world of historical memory and political consequences, which challenge (what Buchloh sees) as the often empty, and self-enclosed sphere of photographic imagery.

The images of the Holocaust victims are particularly poignant, says Buchloh, as they follow an extensive series of consumerist, "popish" imagery. Cut off from any personal or historical referents these advert-like photographs form a part of the simulacral economy of the image, producing photographs that are always already known and yet are continuously novel. It is within this context of the self-enclosed and circulatory system of image production and exchange that the imagery of the Holocaust, says Buchloh, may still offer us a link to what was, but no longer is "out there."

The revelation of the lingering link between the photographic image and the world "out there" highlights however, not only the potential ties between the photograph and its referents, but also the precariousness of these ties and the anxiety surrounding their preservation. The use of trauma to assert a meaning for what otherwise may be a vacant image, may indeed be successful in securing the link between the image and referent, but the traumatic is also that which evades

representation altogether and remains a perpetually missed encounter—undermining the stability of the very link it establishes.[10] It is thus the image-referent relations follow the trajectory of the traumatic event itself, continuously re-performing the (post) traumatic memory while evading the more direct access of language and discourse.

Buchloh's reading of the archive is inextricably linked with his understanding of the photograph and the amassment of photographic images as working to banish the trauma of the real. Quoting Siegfried Kracauer, Buchloh writes that "what photographs, by their sheer accumulation attempt to banish is the recollection of death, which is part and parcel of every memory image...the real vanishes and becomes an allegory of death" (Buchloh 2000: 11). Unlike Iversen's approach then, in which the photograph is very much a part of an ongoing event that may be followed and recorded (if not arrested), the "Buchlohian" photographic image is constructed as a fetish of the lost object. Much like Roland Barthes, Buchloh sees the photograph as working to expel the dead while recalling its presence, and as for Barthes the significance of the photograph for Buchloh often hinges on the mechanism of the traumatic.

It is interesting to compare Buchloh's approach to the traumatic, as it pans out in Richter's work, to that of Renée Green. Like Richter, Green addresses painful historical events, such as the shooting at Kent State University (albeit on a different magnitude); but however important these events are, both historically and in her work, they never seem to serve as the traumatic crux of her installations, as they do in Richter's *Atlas* and Buchloh's reading of it. Rather than a revelation of the last remaining link between the image and its referent, one which stands in stark opposition to the vacant consumerist imagery, Green's documentary images, as well as the text and audio documents included in her work, form a complex web of relations between events and representations that are both personal and historical, idiosyncratic and socially significant. Thus the shooting at Kent State, addressed in Green's work *Partially Buried in Three Parts*, does not remain an isolated if crucially important event in the work, but is linked to Green's own familial history, as well as much wider aspects of American history, including the US relations with both Germany and Korea.

It is Hal Foster's essay on the archive, "An Archival Impulse," that addresses such "relational" and performative archives as found in Green's work (Foster 2004). Foster traces the recent changes in archival practices as well as the archive's growing appeal, and refers to Buchloh's essay on Richter's *Atlas* as well as the work of Renée Green and Thomas Hirschhorn discussed here. Like Jan Verwoert, Foster distinguishes between archival projects, such as Boltanski's and Richter's, in which the link between the image and the historico-political event is secured through the traumatic, and projects for which a plethora of such links, rather than a singularly traumatic one, exist. The more contemporary and "relational" archival projects, says Foster, "propos[e] new orders of affective association, however partial and provisional" and acknowledge their limited ability (or desire) to link firmly a singular event to specific images. Rather than searching for such affirmative associations, they prefer to focus on forging significant historical, political and aesthetics

links between numerous events and their multifaceted representations" (Foster 2004: 21).

Considering the social and political aspects of such "relational" archives, it is possible, as Foster suggests, that their ambition to link various and often-disparate events and images may lead to a rather hermetic and idiosyncratic practice that "betray[s] a hint of paranoia." "For what is paranoia" says Foster "if not a practice of forced connections and bad combinations, of my own private archive, of my own notes from the underground, put on display?" (Foster 2004: 21). But, although such partial and personal archives as Green's may indeed face the danger of recoiling into a subjective and politically redundant haven of paranoid association, the "paranoid dimension of archival art" says Foster is perhaps "the other side of [the archival work's] utopian ambition—its desire to turn belatedness into becomingness, to recoup failed visions in art, literature, philosophy, and everyday life into possible scenarios of alternative kinds of social relations, to transform *the no-place of the archive into the no-place of a utopia*" (Foster 2004: 22; emphasis added). The archive, suggests Foster, may be becoming the new "test site" for alternative social relations, one in which the implications of historical events, even traumatic ones, may be considered within a web of relations, rather than serve as the last vestige of historically and politically significant imagery. For if the archive is becoming the no-place site of utopia (a site which has not featured prominently in the last decades), existing documents and images may be used not only as a testimony to what has happened, but as grounds for considering what may be one day, both aesthetically and politically. It is within the changing paradigm of the archive, from an "excavation site" to a "construction site," that our concepts of documentation and photography may also be reconsidered. For as a part of the "shift away from a melancholic culture that views the historical as little more than the traumatic" as Foster says, towards an archival practice which renewed vigor in re-imagining our political horizons, documentation may find once again a role that is not divorced from the political and historical world "out there," without resorting to the traumatic assertion of the image and its referent (Foster 2004: 22).

Acknowledgments

I would like to thank the Nicolai Wallner Gallery in Denmark, which very kindly provided a copy of Villesen's video art works for the purposes of this research.

Notes

1 A few of the existing texts addressing these issues will be mentioned throughout this essay. However two of the earlier texts published at the beginning of this decade, which I have not specifically addressed here, although they have informed my thinking on the subject are Durden and Richardson (2000) and Kaye (2000).

2 The *Import/Export Funk Office* has been well documented and discussed in several catalogs, websites, and essays, to an extent that I could not re-create in the limited scope of this article. See, for example, Bruno et al. (1999), Cruz and Nickas (1997), Leung (2001). A web-based documentation of this exhibition can be found at http://www.mcachicago.org/MCA/exhibit/past/anxiety/green.html.

3 The concept of Green's *Import/Export Funk Office* as well as its historical and didactic dimensions refer directly to Adrian Piper's *Funk Lessons*

(1982–4). See Piper's description of the work in Piper (1996: 195–216).

4 Hirschhorn's comments have been quoted and discussed by several critics. See for example Pacquement (2004) and Garrett (2004).

5 See Barthes' own writing on photography in Barthes (1982). Iversen herself has discussed Barthes' conceptualization of photography before (Iversen 1994).

6 An earlier version of this essay appeared in Crimp (1977).

7 Gitte Villesen's work has been discussed in the following essays: Bæhrenz (1998), Bourriaud (1998), Heiser and Verwoert (2004), and Olsen (1999).

8 I would like to thank the Cultural Computer Science Institute of the University of Lüneburg which very kindly provided me with information on and a copy of Green's digital version of the *Import/Export Funk Office* for the purpose of this research.

9 Although Buchloh does not reference Rosalind's Krauss' writing on the grid explicitly, her work on this subject is relevant to understanding both Buchloh's own work and more directly the work of the artists mentioned here. See Krauss (1980, 1985).

10 The complex connections between photography and trauma, and more specifically the imaging of the Holocaust have been profoundly discussed in Ulrich Baer's (2002) book on the subject.

References

Bæhrenz, L. 1998. *Addicted to Stories*. Odense, Denmark: Musset for fotokunst, Brandts Klædefabrik.

Baer, U. 2002. *Spectral Evidence: The Photography of Trauma*. Cambridge, MA: MIT Press.

Barthes, R. 1982. *Camera Lucida: Reflections on Photography*. Trans. R. Howard. London: Jonathan Cape.

Bishop, C. 2006. "The Social Turn: Collaboration and Its Discontents." *Artforum* XLIV(6): 178–84.

Bourriaud, N. 1998. *Relational Aesthetics*. Trans. S. Pleasance and F. Woods. Dijon: Les Presses du Reel.

Bruno G., Eng, M., Green, R., Tillman, L. and Wood, J. 1999. *Renée Green: Between and Including*, exhibition catalog. Vienna: Secession Gallery.

Buchloh, B. 2000. "Gerhard Richter's Atlas: The Anomic Archive." In B.H.D. Buchloh, J.F. Chevrier, A. Zweite and A.R. Rochlitz (eds) *Photography and Painting in the Work of Gerhard Richter*, pp. 11–31. Barcelona: MACBA.

Crimp, D. 1977. *Pictures*, exhibition catalog. New York: Artists Space.

Crimp, D. 1980. "The Photographic Activity of Postmodernism." *October* 15: 91–101.

Crimp, D. 1995. "The Photographic Activity of Postmodernism (reprint)." In *On the Museum's Ruins*, pp. 108–26. Cambridge, MA: MIT Press.

Cruz, A. and Nickas, R. 1997. *Performance Anxiety*. Chicago, IL: Museum of Contemporary Art.

Durden, M. and Richardson, C. 2000. *Face On: Photography as a Social Exchange*. London: Black Dog Publishing.

Foster, H. 2004. "An Archival Impulse." *October* 110: 3–22.

Garrett, C. 2004. "Philosophical Battery." *Flash Art* 238.

Green, R. "Site Specificity Unbound: Considering Participatory Mobility." *Cepa Journal* Winter–Spring: 1–5.

Heiser, J. and Verwoert, J. 2004. "What's the Difference: Discussing the Relationship between Art and Documentry Filmmaking with Artists Yael Bartana, Annika Eriksson, Anri Sala and Gitte Villesen." *Frieze* 84. http://www.frieze.com/issue/article/whats_the_difference/, accessed September 2008.

Hirschhorn, T. 2003. Lecture. Bristol, Arnolfini Museum, November 2003. http://www.situations.org.uk/pdfs/lecture_archive_document.pdf, accessed September 2008.

Iversen, M. 1994. "What Is a Photograph?" *Art History* 17: 450–64.

Iversen, M. 2006. "Following Pieces: On Performative Photography." In J. Elkins (ed.) *Photography Theory*, pp. 91–109. London: Routledge.

James, S. 2006. "The Truth about Photography." *Art Monthly* 292: 7–10.

Kaye, N. 2000. *Site Specific Art: Performance, Place and Documentation*. London: Routledge.

Krauss, R. 1980. *Grids: Format and Image in 20th Century Art*, exhibition catalog. New York: The Pace Gallery.

Krauss, R. (ed.). 1985. "Grids." In *The Originality of the Avant Garde and Other Modern Myths*, pp. 8–23. Cambridge, MA: MIT Press.

Leung, S. "Contemporary Returns to Conceptual Art: Renée Green, Silvia Kolbowski, and Stephen Prina." *Art Journal* 60(2): 54–71.

Lind, M. 2004. *The Actualization of Space* (October 2004). http://www.republicart.net/disc/aap/lind01_en.htm, accessed September 2008.

Olsen, S.K. 1999. *Gitte Villesen*. Vienna: Secession Publishing.

Owens, C. 1984. "The Allegorical Impulse: Towards a Theory of Postmodernism." In B. Wallis (ed.) *Art after Modernism: Rethinking Representation*, pp. 52–88. New York: Godine.

Pacquement, A. 2004. "The Precarious Museum." *Tate Etc.* 2. http://www.tate.org.uk/tateetc/issue2/precariousmuseum.htm, accessed September 2008.

Phelan, P. 1993. *Unmarked: The Politics of Performance*. London: Routledge.

Piper, A. 1996. *Out of Order Out of Sight*, Vol. I, pp. 195–216. Cambridge, MA: MIT Press.

Van Duyn E. (ed.). 1996. *Certain Miscellanies—Some Documents*, pp. 70–92. Amsterdam: De Appel Foundation.

Verwoert, J. 2003. "Research and Display: Of Transformations of Documentary Practice in Recent Art." In G. Neuerer (ed.) *Untitled (Experience of Place)*, pp. 9–23. London: Koenig Books.

**Photography
& Culture**

Volume 2—Issue 2
July 2009
pp. 171–182
DOI:

10.2752/175145109X12456654102803

Review Essay

Rereading the History of Photography

The Photobook: A History, **Martin Parr and Gerry
Badger. Vol. I. London: Phaidon Press. 2004. 320pp.
£45.00.**

The Photobook: A History, **Martin Parr and Gerry
Badger. Vol. II. London: Phaidon Press. 2006. 336pp.
£45.00.**

Reviewed by Lucy Mulroney

Lucy Mulroney is a PhD student in the Visual and Cultural
Studies Program at the University of Rochester where she
studies the history of the book, theories of reading and
fiction, and the role of publishing within contemporary visual
arts practices. Her writing has been published in *Artweek*, *Art
Review*, and *caa.reviews*.

In 1855 the London print seller Thomas Agnew & Sons
financed the photographer for the British Royal Family,
Roger Fenton, to photograph the war being waged against
the Russians in the Crimea. Despite the fact that Agnew's
commission was a commercial one, Queen Victoria
and Prince Albert supported the project perhaps out
of concern for the increasingly mismanaged war, which
was being fiercely criticized by the London *Times* war
correspondent William Howard Russell.[1] After touring for
three months in the Crimea, Fenton returned to London
with over 350 photographs—none of which portrayed
the horrific realities of war, but instead showed panoramic
landscapes and portraits of officers. Whether there was an
explicit agreement among Agnew, Fenton, and the British
government about the expected tone and content of
Fenton's photographs is unknown; in any event, after the war
ended with the fall of Sevastopol in September 1855, the
same month that Fenton's photographs were first exhibited
in London, the public's interest in them rapidly petered out.
By December of 1856 Thomas Agnew & Sons sold their

entire holdings of Fenton's sets, prints, and negatives at auction. Despite the brevity of their popularity, these photographs have something to teach us about the complexity of the photographic image. Fenton's Crimean War photographs reveal that multiple and often simultaneous recontextualizations are vital to any history of photography.

During the period when Fenton's photographs garnered popular interest they circulated in a variety of modes. They were exhibited at galleries in London and Paris. They were reproduced as wood engravings in the *Illustrated London News*. They were published as individual mounted prints sold separately and in sets organized by topics such as "incidents of camp life" and "historical portraits." And in 1856 a selection of 160 of them was published as a "complete work" under the title *Photographs Taken Under the Patronage of Her Majesty the Queen in the Crimea by Roger Fenton Esq* (Parr and Badger 2004: 43). Each of the contexts in which Fenton's photographs existed provided a different relationship between the viewer and the image—sometimes personal, tactile, and proprietary, other times distanced, aestheticized, public—and therefore each elicited a different way of reading the images.

In our current moment of shifting regimes of communication technologies an awareness of how texts and images fluctuate across different contexts is inescapable. The growing influence of online publishing and electronic reading devices threatens traditional ideas about reading and the role of books in society. At the same time, a similar shift changes the terrain of photography. As the digital photograph replaces film, electronic means of storing, publishing, and sharing images steadily

replace traditional modes of archiving and dissemination. In order to envision the repercussions of this digital turn we must consider how context has played a role in the meaning of texts and images historically. It is no coincidence then at this transitional moment for both printed texts and photographic images that many scholars have turned to examine the history of the relationship between the photograph and the printed page.

One of the most recent reassessments of this relationship is Martin Parr and Gerry Badger's weighty two-volume *The Photobook: A History* (2004, 2006) in which they retell the history of the photographic medium through the history of the book. In the presentation and discussion of nearly 450 photographically illustrated books, which range in publication date from the 1840s to 2005 and in geographic origin from Leningrad to Little Rock, and from Argentina to Czechoslovakia, Parr and Badger's *The Photobook*, reveals a rich and international vein of photographic history that has often remained untapped, or simply ignored, by art historians. Yet Parr and Badger's project is decidedly not an art historical one. Instead, their survey, in their view, remains true to the impossibility of a singular shared history of photography (Parr and Badger 2004: 6).

As such *The Photobook* unabashedly sidesteps the singular photograph. The personal snapshot is missing; the magazine page, even the family photo album are all left outside the parameters of Parr and Badger's history. Rather than provide a comprehensive narrative for the history of photography Parr and Badger's *The Photobook* performs two main tasks. The first is to "narrate a new history of photography through the specific story of the photobook," which will address the aesthetic, technological, and socio-political in equal measure (Parr and Badger 2004: 5–6). The second task is to define the criteria for what exactly constitutes a "photobook," which Parr and Badger contend is something different from the usual photographically illustrated book or photographer's monograph.

In order to accomplish their first task, the authors have bisected their history into two volumes, each following its own approach. Volume I is roughly chronological. It surveys photobooks published between the years of 1843 and 2001 in order to reinscribe the work of familiar photographers such as William Henry Fox Talbot, Jacob Riis, and Alexander Gardner into the material structure of the books where much of their work was first seen. Volume II is thematic in approach. It looks at genres of photobooks in order to reveal a number of overlooked trajectories in photography's history including the high school yearbook, commercial publications, and artists' books. In sum, Parr and Badger offer a counter narrative to both the mass medium history and the fine art history of photography by emphasizing the integral role of bookmaking and publishing to photographic practices since the advent of the medium. Perhaps more persuasive than any one example in proving the importance of the relationship between the photograph and the book is the cumulative mass of recognizable images reproduced as existing within the material structure of the codex. That is, Parr and Badger manage to accomplish their point in the most simple, yet undoubtedly expensive, way: the illustrations. Beautiful color reproductions fill page after page of *The Photobook*. With or without

text or captions, bound in blue leather or in red cloth, Parr and Badger show the photographic image as being part of the materiality of the book. The technique is effective: even the most familiar of images begins to look a little different in this context.

The authors' second task of defining the "photobook" is a bit trickier to accomplish. In claiming that the photobook is an autonomous art form, unique and different from the usual book illustrated with photographs, Parr and Badger perpetuate a type of aesthetically legitimizing discourse. "This study focuses on a specific kind of photobook and a particular breed of photobook producer. The photographer/ author has been considered here as auteur …" (Parr and Badger 2004: 6–7). Consequently Parr and Badger insert their history into one of the enduring debates of photo-history, which they characterize as the "dance by photographers round the totem pole of auteurship" (Parr and Badger 2004: 11). It's true, the question is as pervasive as it is old: what is the status of the photographer? Is the photographer an artist? A journalist? A cog in a propaganda machine? Perhaps he or she is a civic employee, a member of the military, a scientist, or a doctor. What about the anonymous photographer? Do any of these categorizations of the photographing subject exclude the possibility of the other?

While Parr and Badger insist that the focus of their study is not on "art-photography" they claim that the author of the photobook must be understood as an "auteur" and that the photobook is "an important form in its own right" (Parr and Badger 2004: 9, 7). This stance has two important consequences for their study. First, it gives the "author" of the photobook, regardless of whether she or he is a photographer or an editor appropriating found photographs, an equally elevated and aesthetically defined status. Second, it designates the photobook as a complete and hermetic object that is the product of the "auteur's" vision. In their attempt to legitimate the photobook as an "object in itself," Parr and Badger construct a paradox at the foundation of their survey. The photobook, they explain, "resides at a vital interstice between the art and the mass medium, between the journeyman and the artist, between the aesthetic and the contextual" (Parr and Badger 2004: 11). But they do not allow the photobook to remain in this eternally in-between space. Instead Parr and Badger argue for its aesthetic status: "The photobook is, in short, the literary novel amongst photographic books" (Parr and Badger 2004: 8). So while they critique the "imbalance in favor of the aesthetic" in the histories of photography, Parr and Badger cast the photobook in that same light (Parr and Badger 2004: 6). By emphasizing that these books are "art," Parr and Badger de-emphasize the roles that the photobooks play within a global matrix of books and readers.

In addition to being the product of an auteur, Parr and Badger delineate additional criteria for the photobook. It must have a "theme," its "primary message must be carried by the photographs," it should have a distinct "voice," it should have "intent," it is an object in which "the collective meaning is more important that the images' individual meanings" (Parr and Badger 2004: 7–9). Yet Parr and Badger also qualify these criteria: the photobook can be made without intent, it can be made by someone who is not a

photographer, it can be made by a yearbook committee or a government agency, it can be completely devoid of photographic images. Parr and Badger's development of criteria for photobooks and their immediate self-contradiction of these criteria are simultaneously the source of my critique and my favorite part of *The Photobook*. Parr and Badger fail to follow their own rules. The contours of their study self destruct, thereby revealing the frivolity of constructing such categories. What really is the difference between the "photobook" and the "photographically illustrated book"? Is there any significance in distinguishing between the "artist's book" and the "artist's photobook"? What about the edited artist's book of found photographs made on commission? Why insist upon the "auteur"? Do any of these labels help us better understand these objects in any way? Or are they just the product of scholars and artists trying to stake their claim before anyone has really struck gold?

Parr and Badger acknowledge the failure of their criteria. After identifying, delineating, and hierarchizing their subject, they defend their contradictions by taking an anti-academic stance. They write: "Whatever the feelings of those purists who like to pigeonhole areas of photographic practice into a neatly categorized view of photo history, the photobook just does not work like that. If this book seems wayward and discursive at times, it is only reflecting its subject's baffling diversity, and the difficulty of telling a smooth, homogenized story with no loose ends and contradictions" (Parr and Badger 2006: 6). This is an unconvincing argument when it follows the authors' attempts to legitimatize their subject aesthetically through the explication of a set of criteria for it. To that end, although Parr and Badger's argument for the art status of the photobook seemingly conflicts with their calls for acknowledging context, the hundreds of examples of photobooks they provide do reveal a blind spot in the traditional narratives of photography that remain rooted within the discourse of art history. The more important question becomes not how do we reclaim the photobook as art, but why has art history ignored this area of photographic practice and what are the ramifications of this exclusion?

A quick perusal of recent art history surveys suggests that Parr and Badger may be correct in their assertion that the photobook resides, for the most part, beyond the charted territory of photo scholarship. For example, in the most recent edition of the classic *Janson's History of Art* (2007) the reproductions of a Carleton E. Watkins photograph of Yosemite, a Timothy O'Sullivan Civil War battlefield photograph, and John Thomson's iconic portrait of a homeless woman are each cropped so closely that any hint that these images were book illustrations is completely lost (Davies 2007: 894–5). Marilyn Stokstad's survey, *Art History* (2008), reproduces a tightly cropped Jacob Riis photograph, mentioning that it was published in *How the Other Half Lives* but leaving out the fact that text accompanied this photograph and that it was in one of the first books to use halftone photographic reproductions extensively (Stokstad 2008: 796). As Parr and Badger point out, since the birth of representational theories and visual cultural studies, scholars have acknowledged the importance of an image's context more

regularly (Parr and Badger 2004: 6). But even the recent theory-oriented survey *Art Since 1900,* which claims to "provide the most comprehensive critical history of art in the twentieth and early twenty-first centuries ever published," neglects to reproduce the examples of photography as anything other than aestheticized and singular prints—the only exception to this being the reproduction of Ed Ruscha's photographically illustrated artist's book: *Every Building on the Sunset Strip* (Foster, Krauss, Bois and Buchloh, 2004: 507).[2] Even in what is probably the most well-known photography survey text, Beaumont Newhall's *The History of Photography* (1982), the reproductions show the history of photography as a history of images, rather than a history of images printed on glass or metal and then stored in little leather cases, or of images printed on paper and then mounted and bound in books. On the other hand, Michel Braive's *The Photograph: A Social History* (1966), Gisèle Freund's *Photography and Society* (1980), and more recently Geoffrey Batchen's *Each Wild Idea: Writing, Photography, History* (2001) are noteworthy examples of photo histories that pay close attention to the social context of the photographic image. Yet the specific history of photographically illustrated books lies outside the focus of each of these texts.

Recently a number of scholars have engaged directly with different aspects of the relationship between photographic image and the page.[3] Some, like Renée Riese Hubert, Johanna Drucker, and Cornelia Lauf have concentrated on the idea of the artist's book, whereas others like Harold Evans and Robert Lebeck have addressed the history of photojournalism.[4] In 1999 Museo Nacional Centro de Arte Reina

Sofia in Madrid published a hefty survey to accompany the exhibition *Fotografía Pública: Photography in Print 1919–1939*. Focusing on the intense period of photographic invention that occurred in the interwar period, this catalogue investigates how artists used mass media to develop an international photographic language for both aesthetic and functional purposes (Cabrera in Fernández 1999: 9). Featuring reproductions of photographic works contextualized within material objects such as posters, magazines, and books, *Fotografía Pública* is a flush compendium of a crucial moment in photo history. Carol Armstrong's 1998 study, *Scenes in a Library: Reading the Photograph in the Book, 1843–1875*, addresses the photographically illustrated book specifically, and aims to reverse the way that the verbal framing of the photograph has become invisible (Armstrong 1998: 1).[5] Through what she calls "an oscillation between close looking and equally close reading," Armstrong works to reinscribe photographs by nineteenth-century British photographers including Anna Atkins, Francis Frith, and Julia Margaret Cameron into their original "textual surround" (Armstrong 1998: 3). Yet while Armstrong's text aims to return these photographs to their place on the page, the closely cropped reproductions in her book neglect to support this effort. Andrew Roth's *The Book of 101 Books: Seminal Photographic Books of the Twentieth Century* (2001) follows a similar course by considering the structure and materiality of the book—paper, binding, typeface, "mise-en-page," and so forth—vitally important to the aesthetic apprehension of the photograph (Roth 2001: 1). Fortunately the reproductions in Roth's survey depart from the common method

of tightly cropping the photographic image, and instead they show us photographs belonging to the material structure of the codex. In this way, Roth's volume offers a new look at key photographic publications such as Alfred Stieglitz's *Camera Work* and Helen Levitt's *A Way of Seeing*. Most recently, *Imagining Paradise: The Richard and Ronay Menschel Library at George Eastman House, Rochester* (2007) has added to this growing engagement with the relationship between book culture and photo history by providing a survey of the library at the George Eastman House, one of the most important and longstanding photography institutions in the United States. This book is particularly significant because it brings technical manuals and historical treatises about the medium of photography into the conversation. Including over 250 books, which are reproduced with particular attention paid to their materiality, *Imagining Paradise* "adds to the historical record" of photography through the portrait of this important library (Foster, Heiting and Stuhlman 2007: 9).

While the increasing number of works on the shared history of publishing and photography reveal that this is a rapidly growing area of critical interest, an important caveat also emerges. Pulling books or other printed materials out of their particular socio-cultural contexts and reclassifying them as "photo-works" provides only a partial representation that risks obscuring other aspects of the these objects' historically and culturally contingent meanings. How best to negotiate the duality of an object's aesthetic status and its cultural and historical specificity remains open to interrogation. *The Photobook* is not exempted from this polemic. On the one hand, Parr and Badger cast the photobook as an aesthetic object but, on the other hand, by emphasizing photography's place within the cultural history of books, they call forth a whole set of new concerns for the history for photography. Although Parr and Badger rarely engage at any substantial length in their descriptive entries or in their chapter essays with issues of access, literacy, circulation, distribution, translation, and interpretation, the cumulative result of their survey, I believe, is that these topics become indelible to the study of photography's relationship to print culture.

If we are to begin to articulate a history of the cultural meanings of books, we must examine how they are conveyers of not only verbal texts but visual ones as well. Simultaneously, by pursuing a history of photography where the photograph is understood in relationship to the often multiple material structures in which it exists, we can begin to examine the cultural divisions that guide different apprehensions of the same image. Ultimately Parr and Badger's survey, together with the others just mentioned, point us in a new direction—they turn the history of photography towards a history of reading.

Acknowledging the photograph's presentation in the context of a book can change the way we read both the image and the book. This is perhaps the most pertinent, yet implicit, point of Parr and Badger's history. After flipping past a few examples of books by Francis Frith, Karl Blossfeldt, and Lewis Hine, we begin to notice how the differences in the material structure of each book affects the photographs it holds; we begin to see how text and image and paper and binding interact. And, in turn,

we begin to contemplate how and why this book was published, who bought it, and how it circulated. Parr and Badger make evident how the structure of the book affects the meaning of the photograph in their inclusion of the infamous Second World War publication *KZ: Bildbericht aus fünf Konzertrationslagern (Photo Report from Five Concentration Camps)*. A 32-page booklet published by the American War Information Unit, which contained 44 devastating photographs accompanied by a "terse" commentary, *KZ* was dropped by parachute into Germany in 1945. Describing *KZ* as one of the "most poignant photobooks ever published," Parr and Badger explain that it was meant to convey the monstrosity of the war to the German public (Parr and Badger 2004: 194). "Thus this book," Parr and Badger write, "which is not much more than a pamphlet, may represent the single most significant use of photography as a witness in the medium's history" (Parr and Badger 2004: 194). But how do these images function differently within the context of this book than they do on their own? One can hardly imagine how it must have felt to snatch one of these fragile books falling from the sky, only to open it up and find horrific images human bodies tortured and tormented by one's own countrymen. Yet at the same time we can imagine how the images in *KZ* might be recontextualized—as propaganda for the US army or as historical proof for historians of the Holocaust—and thus read differently. As the possession of a German citizen who had just lived through the war, this book would not only have been proof of the atrocities of the war, it would have been a confrontation on a very personal level. The kind of bodily relationship one has to horrific images bound within a book that is small enough to fit into your pocket is very different from the relationship one has to an image of war or torture printed in the newspaper, or streaming across the internet, where there is an ideological distance built into the mode of dissemination. Imagine if little books filled with images of all the horrors of our present war were dropped by parachute into our backyards and across our cities. Would you feel differently about those same images you've seen on the news over recent years if you saw them printed and bound one after another after another in a book accompanied by an accusatory text? You would have to decide whether to keep this book or throw it away. Where would you store such a book in your home?

Sometimes, as Parr and Badger show, contextualizing a photograph within its material structure makes interpreting its meaning more difficult. This is most evident in the chapter "Point of Sale: The Company Photobook" in Volume II where Parr and Badger reveal the tenuous nature of the line that divides the "commercial" from the "fine art" photobook. Most photographers, they argue, work on both sides of the fence: "The bibliography of Henri Cartier-Bresson includes not only *The Decisive Moment* … but a book commissioned by IBM, *Man and Machine*, published in 1969; Josef Koudelka produced not only *Gypsies* … but also *Limestone* (2001), a book made for the French quarry company Groupe Lhoist, on which he worked for two years" (Parr and Badger 2006: 179).

One salient example Parr and Badger provide of an artist working across the commercial versus fine art divide is the book that the Surrealist artist Man Ray produced

in 1931 for La Compagnie parisienne de distribution d'électricité (CPDE). Simply titled *Électricité*, Man Ray's book is stunning in its spare elegance. Produced in a small run of 500, the book is basically a customer appreciation piece. It consists of a die-cut chemise with a black cloth portfolio and slipcase, which holds 10 loose-leaf "rayograms" and an eight-page booklet with modernist typography (Parr and Badger 2006: 182). Man Ray's *Électricité* is dramatic and sensual. His "rayograms" depict the various domestic uses of electricity and they might be some of the most compelling images he ever made. Regardless of whether the CPDE intended to commission an artist's photobook or Man Ray simply intended to make something that would bring in some money, this book operates on both levels. It can be read as a commercial project and as an artistic one. The "intentional fallacy," Parr and Badger point out, is as relevant to photography as it is to literature. "The functional photobook, if executed with consistency and visual intelligence, has the capacity to operate on a different level from that originally envisaged" (Parr and Badger 2004: 9). Therefore Parr and Badger not only show that the commercial projects executed by artists might be art, but they also open the door for all photobooks, whether created by artists or not, to be considered as aesthetic objects.

It is through examples like *KZ* and Man Ray's *Électricité* that Parr and Badger turn the history of photography towards a history of reading. To think about reading is to reflect on how the same "text" can have multiple meanings and how those meanings are guided by the codes of behavior that characterize different communities of readers. Along these lines, the work of Roger Chartier provides a few key entry points. In his essay "Labourers and Voyagers: From the text to the reader," Chartier extends the ideas of the reception theorists out of the abstract realm and into the "concrete" practices of readers. In establishing a starting point for anyone interested in the history of reading, Chartier makes two basic claims: "a text does not exist except for a reader who gives it signification"; and readers "never confront abstract, idealized texts detached from any materiality" (Chartier 2002: 47; 48). Chartier emphasizes that acknowledging the materiality of the text also means acknowledging the behaviors that come along with it. Readers "hold in their hands or perceive objects and forms whose structures and modalities govern their reading or hearing, and consequently the possible comprehension of the text read or heard" (Chartier 2002: 48). Like a text, the photographic image relies on a reader, or in the case of a photobook, a viewer-reader, for its signification. But that space in which the viewer approaches the photograph is always structured. It is structured by the materiality of the photographic image and by the behavioral codes that govern the space in which it is viewed. Whether the photograph is framed in an art museum or printed in a book or published online, each situation in which an image exists changes the possibilities for its interpretation because, as Chartier points out, each situation brings with it its own gestures, habits, and restrictions. *KZ* and *Électricité* have already shown this dynamic at work, but it is a point worth pursuing further. Let us consider a few of the contexts in which Dorothea Lange's famous photograph *Migrant Mother*

has existed: in the press; as a 7 × 9 in. print available for purchase from the Library of Congress gift shop; in the files of the US Farm Security Administration; on t-shirts; on the walls of art museums; as well as in two different photobooks included in Parr and Badger's survey. The first is in the optimistic photobook, *Land of the Free,* compiled by the American poet Archibald MacLeish in 1938. The second is in a sarcastic and damning Nazi photobook *USA—nackt!* created by Erwin Berghaus in 1943 (Parr and Badger 2004: 180). We can imagine how each of these material structures provides a different kind of social space for the image's reception. The t-shirt provides a means of self-identification with this now nostalgic image of American will power. Read within the context of the FSA files the photograph becomes an indexical artifact of the Depression. In the art museum it becomes sadly beautiful. Whereas within the Nazi book that could have been purchased and held in the hands, the image reads as the epitome of despair that is hidden beneath America's false facade.

Obviously a singular history of the meaning of this photograph will not suffice. So rather than conclude that there is one "true" way of reading any photograph, it is more important to follow Chartier towards a history of reading that aims to "reconstruct the variations that differentiate the 'readable space' (the texts in their material and discursive forms) and those which govern the circumstances of their 'actualization' (the readings seen as concrete practices and interpretive procedures)" (Chartier 2002: 48). The photobook, Parr and Badger point out, provides one of those "readable" spaces. And it deserves critical consideration both within the discourse of art history and outside of it.

My only question is: why create a set of parameters that dictates that similar printed contexts should be left out of this history?[6] Why not acknowledge that homemade photo albums could be part of the history of the photobook. Moreover, why not include photocopied publications?[7] Parr and Badger insist that their history is a completely subjective one and that they hope it will spark new and divergent histories. But then why establish criteria beyond this subjective selection, especially when it is not followed? There might be a few answers to this. First, any 656-page, two-volume book full of color reproductions must qualify its subject matter beyond simply "our favorites." Second, the authors, and perhaps their publicists, are trying to differentiate this survey from the other texts on similar subjects. Or third, and my favorite answer, is that Parr and Badger are themselves constructing a photobook. This third option is not so far fetched given Martin Parr's own oeuvre of photobooks that he has published as an internationally recognized photographer.

The outliers in Parr and Badger's study, the books that contradict the conditions they set forth, are in fact where we begin to see what they are trying to prove: that any book can be considered a photobook. The artist's book of haikus without photos and the high school yearbook that is clearly without an "auteur" become photobooks because they are framed within context of Parr and Badger's book. The "auteur" that Parr and Badger insist upon, reveals itself as simply the context—whether material, institutional, theoretical—in which the photograph is

situated. The authors admit as much in their description of *Evidence*, the 1977 photobook of found images edited by Larry Sultan and Mike Mandel.

> Take one photograph and its meaning seems relatively clear—if it is, say, of a parachute stuck to a telegraph pole blowing in the wind, it might seem to be depicting the aftermath of a sky-diving accident. But the qualifications necessary in that brief description indicate that even an obvious interpretation is hardly unequivocal. When you place next to it another image with little apparent connection to the first, the meanings of both pictures can be thrown into confusion. (Parr and Badger 2006: 220)

Whether the photographs in *Evidence* were "thrown together" or "cunningly selected in sequence," Parr and Badger hold that the result for the reader is the same: *Evidence* offers "a visual conundrum of incalculable mystery" (Parr and Badger 2006: 220). This felicitous description of the psychological effects that a single book can have on the careful reader serves equally well as a metaphor for the history of photography as a whole. "Mystery" becomes synonymous with possibility. Pasted into a scrapbook, published in a scientific treatise, or plucked from its original purpose, as say, propaganda, and reinserted into the history of art as a singular, aestheticized print, the photograph continually lends itself to recontextualization and thus the possibility of multiple rereadings.

In this way Parr and Badger's *The Photobook* provides an important addition to the history of photography. It serves not only as a historical survey that begins to bridge, or rather highlight, the "interstice" that exists between "mass medium" and "fine art" photography, but it also provides a bridge between scholarship done in the field of the history of the book and that done in art history. While in some ways itself "a visual conundrum of incalculable mystery", *The Photobook* is nonetheless a helpful reference tool and an important starting point for anyone concerned with the circulation of "texts" and the intersection of publishing and visual culture.

Acknowledgments

I am grateful to Professors Joan Shelley Rubin, Grace Seiberling and Joan Saab for their valuable feedback on this essay.

Notes

1 For a full account of the history of Fenton's Crimean War photographs see "'A New Starting Point': Roger Fenton's Life" in Baldwin, Daniel and Greenough (2004). A slightly different account is set forth in "Roger Fenton Crimean War Photographs" on the Library of Congress's Print's and Photographs Reading Room website (www. loc.gov/rr/print/coll/251_fen.html). The Library of Congress suggests that Agnew proposed that Fenton's photographs would diffuse Russell's criticisms, while Greenough argues that Agnew and Fenton's only intention was to produce a "commercially viable portfolio of photographs" rather than depict the war either positively or negatively and that the Queen and Prince offered their support for this project out of their overall concern about the mismanaged war (19–21). For additional accounts of this history see "A New Form of Communication" in Newhall (1982: 85–115) and Gernsheim and Alison Gernsheim (1954).

2 The publisher's assertion that *Art Since 1900* is the most "comprehensive critical history …" can be found on the Thames & Hudson website (www. thameshudson.co.uk/en/1/9780500238189.mxs).

While a handful of illustrations in *Art Since 1900* are presented with a nod towards materiality, for example the reproduction of a photomontage by Salvador Dalí (249) or the famous portrait of André Malraux standing before his "Museum without Walls" (273), I contend that these reproductions still do not present photographic works in their material context. Ed Ruscha's *Sunset Strip* book is the only reproduction of "photography" *in situ*, but the reason for this is most likely because this object is not considered photography but instead an "artist's book." The overall the treatment of photography within *Art Since 1900* is decontextualized. For example, the photographs of August Sander (272), Eadweard Muybridge (94), Karl Blossfeldt (237), Albert Renger-Patzsch (235) are all visually presented in such a cropped manner that they deny any material context.

3 My knowledge and discussion here of the growing wealth of scholarship done on the relationship between the photograph and the printed page is indebted to the tremendously useful bibliography included at the back of Volume I of Parr and Badger's *The Photobook*, p. 316. In addition, by mentioning in what follows books that are not included in Parr and Badger's bibliography it is my hope to contribute the conceptualization of this growing field.

4 Please see the reference section for full citations of these texts.

5 An important precursor to Armstrong's study and to the other books mentioned in this section is Lucien Goldschmidt and Weston Naef's *The Truthful Lens*, published by the Grolier Club in 1980, which was the first bibliographic survey of books illustrated with original photographs.

6 In the introduction to Volume I, Parr and Badger state: "There is no Alfred Stieglitz, no Edward Weston, no Ansel Adams. Stieglitz's *Camera Work* was omitted because, despite its sumptuous production, it was essentially a magazine" (Parr and Badger 2004: 8). Yet the authors neglect to address how the book affects the photograph differently than a magazine, or why the magazine format should be excluded from this history,

especially since the line that separates journals, chapbooks, magazines, catalogs and books is such a slippery one.

7 The possibility for "photocopied" books to be considered as part of the history of photobooks was brought to my attention by "The Copy of the Treaty between Great Britain and China, 1842," which is described at length by Larry J. Schaaf in Foster, Heiting and Stuhlman (2007: 44–5).

References

Armstrong, C. 1998. *Scenes in a Library: Reading the Photograph in the Book, 1843–1875*. Cambridge, MA: MIT Press.

Baldwin, G., Daniel, Malcolm and Greenough, Sarah. 2004. *All the Mighty World: The Photographs of Roger Fenton, 1853–1860*. New Haven: Yale University Press.

Batchen, G. 2001. *Each Wild Idea: Writing, Photography, History*. Cambridge, MA: MIT Press.

Braive, M. 1966. *The Photograph: A Social History*. New York: McGraw-Hill.

Chartier, R. [2002] 1992. Labourers and Voyagers: From the Text to the Reader. In D. Finkelstein and A. McCleery (eds) *The Book History Reader*. London and New York: Routledge.

Davies, P., Denny, W. B., Hofrichter, F. F., Jacobs, J. F., Roberts, A. M. and Simon, D. L. 2007. *Janson's History of Art: The Western Tradition*. Upper Saddle River, NJ: Pearson Prentice Hall.

Drucker, J. [1994] 2004. *The Century of Artists' Books*. New York: Granary Books.

Evans, H. 1978. *Pictures on a Page: Photojournalism, Graphics, and Picture Editing*, London: Heinemann.

Fernández, H. 1999. *Fotografía Pública: Photography in Print 1919–1939*. Madrid: Museo Nacional Centro de Arte Reina Sofia.

Foster, H., Krauss, R., Bois, Y.-A. and Buchloh, B. 2004. *Art Since 1900: Modernism, Antimodernism, Postmodernism*. New York: Thames & Hudson.

Foster, S., Manfreed, H. and Stuhlman, R. 2007. *Imagining Paradise: The Richard and Ronay Menschel Library at the George Eastman House, Rochester*. Rochester, NY: George Eastman House, and Göttingen: Steidl.

Freund, G. 1980. *Photography and Society*. Boston: David R. Godine.

Gernsheim, H. and Gernsheim, A. 1954. *Roger Fenton, Photographer of the Crimean War: His Photographs and His Letters from the Crimea. With an Essay on His Life and Work*. London: Secker & Warburg.

Goldschmidt, L. and Naef, Weston J. 1980. *The Truthful Lens: A Survey of the Photographically Illustrated Book 1844–1914*. New York: The Grolier Club.

Hubert, R. R. and Hubert, J. D. 1999. *The Cutting Edge of Reading: Artists' Books*. New York: Granary Books.

Lauf, C. and Phillpot, C. 1998. *Artist/Author: Contemporary Artists' Books*. New York: Distributed Art Publishers.

Lebeck, R. and Von Dewitz, B. 2001. *Kiosk: A History of Photojournalism*. Göttingen, Germany: Steidl.

Newhall, B. 1982. *The History of Photography: From 1839 to the Present*. 5th edn. New York: Museum of Modern Art.

Parr, M. and Badger, G. 2004. *The Photobook: A History*. Vol I. London and New York: Phaidon Press.

Parr, M. and Badger, G. 2006. *The Photobook: A History*. Vol II. London and New York: Phaidon Press.

Roth, A. (ed.) 2001. *The Book of 101 Books: Seminal Photographic Books of the Twentieth Century*. New York: PPP Editions, in association with Roth Horowitz LLC.

Stokstad, Marilyn. 2008. *Art History*. 3rd edn. Upper Saddle River, NJ: Pearson Education.

Photography & Culture

Volume 2—Issue 2
July 2009
pp. 183–194
DOI:
10.2752/175145109X12456654102849

Recreated Faces: Facial Disfigurement, Plastic Surgery, Photography and the Great War

Francesca Kubicki

Francesca Kubicki studied for a BA (Hons) in History at Kings College, University of London, in 2008.

Abstract

This article derives from my research at Kings College, University of London and focuses on the rebuilding of the faces of British and Commonwealth personnel that were brutally disfigured by the violence of the Great War. The resulting reconstructive surgery was spearheaded by the New Zealander Harold Gillies (1882–1960). A pioneer in the field, Gillies was the main driving force behind the British response to this problem and went on to become the most prominent plastic surgeon in the interwar period. Artists, sculptors and photographers were a fundamental part of the process. They documented the injuries and surgical repair and had an important influence over the aesthetics of the soldier's reformed faces. The whole operation was highly innovative, each problem addressed and overcome with a mixture of skill, creativity and luck. This story is retold by the photographs that fill Gillies' 1920 textbook, *Plastic Surgery of the Face; Based on Selected Cases of War Injuries.* They portray the horrors, triumphs and processes that the men and their faces went through with a stark truth that words could never compete with. Archived photographs used in this research are pivotal to help us to understand the extreme physical interventions and trauma that these men endured. Moreover, these photos act as signifiers of the devastating effects of weaponry and war to the face and the cost to human existence. This creative and highly innovative surgery provokes one to ask what was so significant about this form of mutilation that it created a series of exceptional and fascinating responses. The face has the unique position of being central to how we communicate, and forms a crucial part of our identity, a visual representation of the self, the significance of which cannot be underestimated. Mutilation is therefore particularly abhorrent, and the images of these violated faces create a deeper understanding of the horror of war.

Keywords: history, portraiture, surgery, trauma, war

Defaced

Facial injuries were common in the First World War: the product of a unique set of circumstances. Trench warfare often left the neck and head vulnerable, a risk intensified by men peeking their heads over the parapet, making them a target for a sniper's bullet (Bamji 1996: 490). Mutilation was also a product of new weapons used such as artillery fire, hand grenades and guns. The close proximity of the trenches meant that the bullets did not only pierce the body but shattered it, leaving large entry wounds (Bamji 1996: 490). Gillies noted that the worst form of disfigurement, and the hardest to treat, was the damage wreaked by missiles that tore away large "facial hunks" (Gillies and Millard 1957: 13). A sense of this destruction is given by Sister Catherine Black's description of a man: "who had half his face literally blown to pieces with the skin left hanging in shreds, and the jaw-bones crushed to a pulp that felt like sand under your fingers" (Black 1939: 86). The mortality

rate of such wounds was minimized by the change from soft caps to steel helmets in 1916 (*Lancet*, December 30, 1916: 1109). However, these helmets increased facial mutilation as fragments of the helmets and the projectiles that shattered them often hit the men's bare faces (Haiken 1997: 29).

Deformity was often amplified by the fact that many surgeons did not know how to treat these wounds. Many were "embarrassed" by facial injuries and often closed them up and hoped for the best (Pound 1964: 26). The practice of leaving wounds to heal or simply joining the wound's edges together often led to tight contorted faces, damaging further the recognizable form of the human face. What remained of the human visage can only be described as "hideous" as Ward Muir, an orderly at London Third General Hospital, observed.

> Hideous is the only word left for these smashed faces: the socket with some twisted, moist slit, with a lash or two adhering feebly, which is all that is traceable of the forfeited eye; the skewed mouth which sometimes—in spite of brilliant dentistry contrivances—results from the loss of jaw; and worse, far the worst, the incredibly brutalizing effects which are the consequence of wounds in the nose, and which the climax of mournful grotesquerie when the nose is missing altogether. (Muir 1918: 143–4)

Recreated

Harold Gillies created the specialist unit for facial wounds in 1916 at the Cambridge Military Hospital, Aldershot, as a response to the horrific facial injuries he witnessed working for the Red Cross on the Western

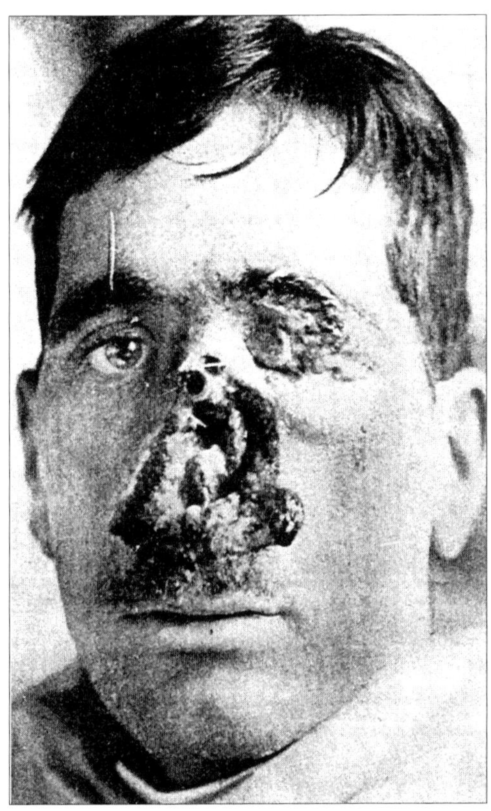

Fig 1 Facial injury—as received in hospital. From Gillies (1920: 289).

Front (Gillies and Millard 1957: 6). This expertise was in great demand and it was soon clear that the 200 beds in Aldershot would not suffice. In 1917, Queen's Hospital, Sidcup was set up to care for this specific demand. Between 1917 and 1925, 11,000 operations were performed and 5,000 service men were treated at Sidcup and associate hospitals (Bamji 1996: 495).

From the medical texts, Gillies' files and others descriptions it is hard to get a real sense of what these patients went through.

Perhaps it is too easy to be in awe of the "progress" of science as these faces were rebuilt, leaving it hard to empathize with the reality of living through the process. It is clear however that three factors—the length of the treatment, its intrusive and painful nature and the absence of antibiotics—made these operations very difficult to bear.

The length of treatment varied but often spanned a period of one to two years (*Lancet,* November 3, 1917: 689). The basis for this is perhaps best expressed by Gillies' maxim: "never do today what can honourably be put off till tomorrow" (Bamji 2006: 155). Each stage of the operations needed to have fully healed before the next could begin. The operations were therefore punctuated by long convalescent periods. Case 364 of a burnt naval officer from Gillies (1920: 360) gives a sense of the painful and lengthy nature of treatment. The first stage of this operation, which took place on the November 12, 1917, is shown by the photograph (Figure 2) where the pedicles (skin flaps used to keep transferred tissue alive) and skin graft are loosened from the body. The next stage, where the old scar tissue was removed and the graft was attached, did not take place until November 30, 1917 (Figure 3). Following this operation the patient suffered considerable infection and the pedicles could not then be removed until January 8, 1918. Only in July 1918, seven months after the first procedure, did the final operation take place (Figure 4) (Gillies 1920: 361).

Although treatment was difficult and its speed and success were heavily influenced by demands on the department's resources, the results were highly impressive (Feo 2007: 20). Procedures were experimental and

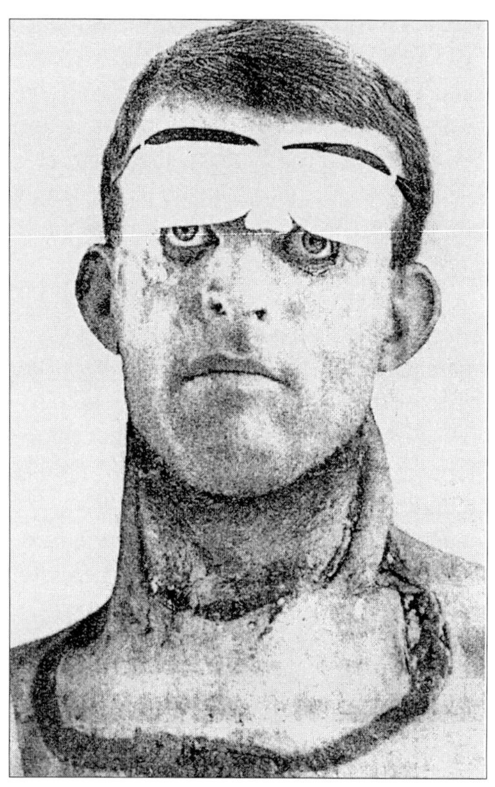

Fig 2 First stage of operation, from Gillies (1920: 362).

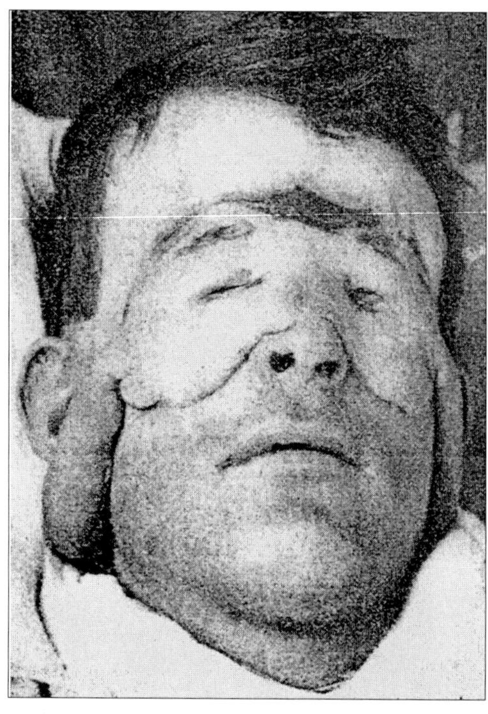

Fig 3 Second stage of operation, from Gillies (1920: 362).

innovative, responding constantly to new injuries and discoveries. Gillies' and his team's feats are even more spectacular considering the absence of antibiotics. Almost all the wounds they received were infected and received the same treatment of being flushed through with sterile water (Bamji 1996: 499). The stages of surgery were also vulnerable to infection as the earlier case describes. Infections posed a great risk to Gillies' work, ruining grafts and causing scarring. An example of this can be seen in a rebuilt nose, Case 517 (Figure 5). The damage caused by infection is just visible in the form of the

nose's wrinkled tip. What the black and white photograph does not show is that the damage was in fact blue, as described in Gillies' notes (Gillies 1920: 288).

As the evidence suggests, living through procedure after procedure was physically and psychologically tough. For some, such as the young man in (Figure 4), it was too much. Many declined to finish their treatment as the lengthy, painful procedures became too difficult to endure, even if good results were likely. The young man pictured is the perfect example of such a case. His misshapen mouth depicts that his series of surgeries was

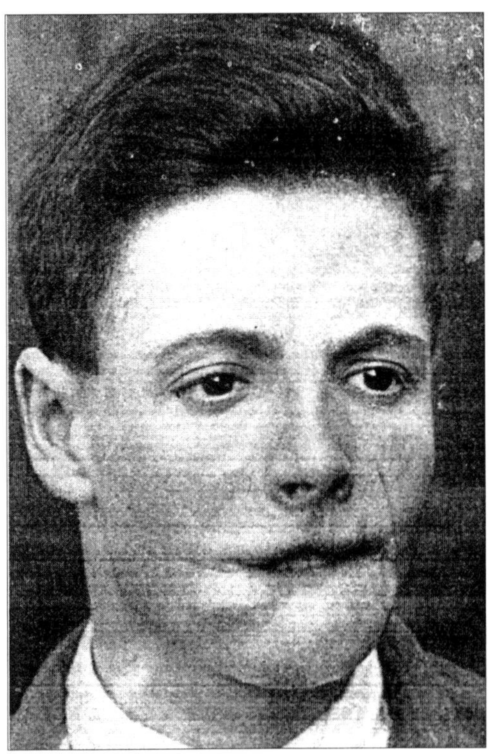

Fig 4 Final (patient refused further treatment), from Gillies (1920: 145).

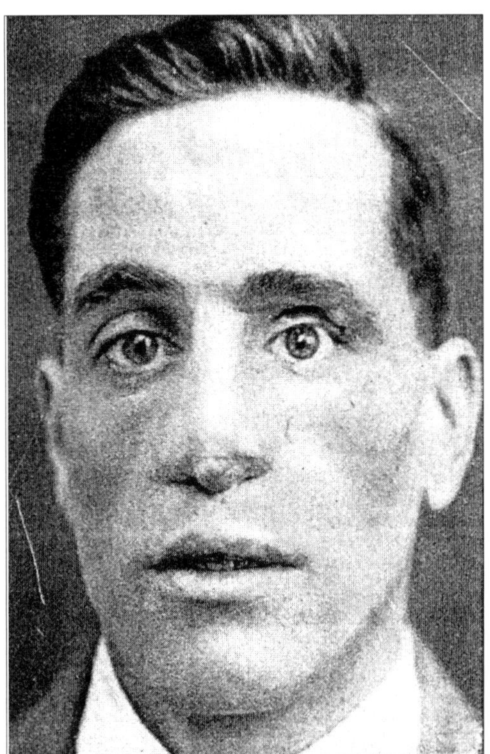

Fig 5 Nose defect, from Gillies (1920: 289).

not yet complete but as Gillies' notes inform us he refused further treatment, choosing to live with this disfigurement—something Gillies found "regrettable" (Gillies 1920: 44).

Photographic evidence such as the sources used in this article are particularly significant in learning about the procedures, and understanding the methods that were used. It captures in detail a brutal reality that would otherwise be difficult to imagine. The photographs allow us to look at the work of Gillies and his team without superimposing our modern ideas of reconstructive surgery. One can see how the results could be incredibly impressive but also how they

could fail to blend in as "normal" features, or go wrong, such as the nose's wrinkled tip. Although some of the work done seems in stark contrast to the faces created by modern reconstructive surgery, the difference compared to what these faces would have looked like was spectacular. These rebuilt faces served their function well and, importantly, allowed these men to perhaps go unnoticed, at least until close inspection.

Facial Masks

Though what could be done for these men was impressive, Gillies and his team could not deal with all injuries, especially substantial loss of tissue. In these cases the next step was to give the men a thin metal mask to disguise, or lessen the visible impact of the injury. These masks were made at three centers: Sidcup, Paris (for French veterans by the American sculptor Anna Coleman) (Feo 2007: 22) and the "Tin Noses Shop," or to use its formal title: the Masks for Facial Disfigurement Department in the Third London General Hospital, which was run by the sculptor Francis Derwent Wood, an orderly at the hospital, who soon found that his creative talent could be put to more particular use (Muir 1918: 146–147). Although masks had been used previously to aid individuals who were disfigured, Katherine Feo notes that the Great War was the first time they had been mass produced as a remedy to the havoc that war wreaked on the soldiers (Feo 2007: 19).

A description of the process that Wood employed and what the department was like can be found in *The Happy Hospital* (1918) by Ward Muir. Muir, who also was an orderly at the hospital, explains that a series of negative and positive casts were made which yielded the basis of the mask. Using a pre-injury photograph Wood would build up the mask to recreate the lost features. The mask would then be created by an electroplate 1/32nd of an inch thick, which Muir (1918: 151) describes as having "a remote resemblance to an irregular bit cut out of one of those papier-mâché vizors worn by revellers at a fancy-dress ball." Finally the plate was covered in a thin layer of silver, and painted to match the patients' skin tones exactly. Muir (1918: 151) describes the department as "fanatically particular." So careful were the department in this process

that commercial artificial eyes were rejected because "faultless pairing … Was seldom achieved." They were replaced instead by painted glass discs. Oil paints and metallic foil eyelashes were used to fill out the features and finally spectacles were soldered to the mask to keep it in place. Spectacles were generally used to secure the mask although some of the smaller ones could be adhered by spirit-gum (Figure 6) (Wood 1917: 949).

Masks would hide the worst of the disfigurement, but their effect was severely limited. The masks may seem amazing in their life-like realism (Figures 7 and 8) but a black-and-white photo cannot truly convey what they looked like in reality. The downfall of these masks was identified by Muir (1918: 148): "[the patient] is able to emerge with a face which at a few yards' distance is almost a replica of the one he wore before he was wounded." It is this emphasis on "a few yards' distance" that highlights the masks' weakness. Up close they did not suffice as reformed faces. They were still only fragments of metal and could not melt into a man's features to take up the likeness of human flesh. Stiff and set, the masks lacked "animate realism" and so stood apart from the rest of the face and could only hide the disfigurement.

The façade of the mask had a limited time frame as the masks' delicate materials were prone to rust and chipped easily causing the illusion to slowly fade bit by bit (Feo 2007: 24). The success of the masks in covering the wounds was also limited; the masks themselves became symbols of the horror that lay underneath (Feo 2007: 18). They took on the metaphor of tragedy, as they infer disfigurement by the fact they were worn. This horror is depicted by the

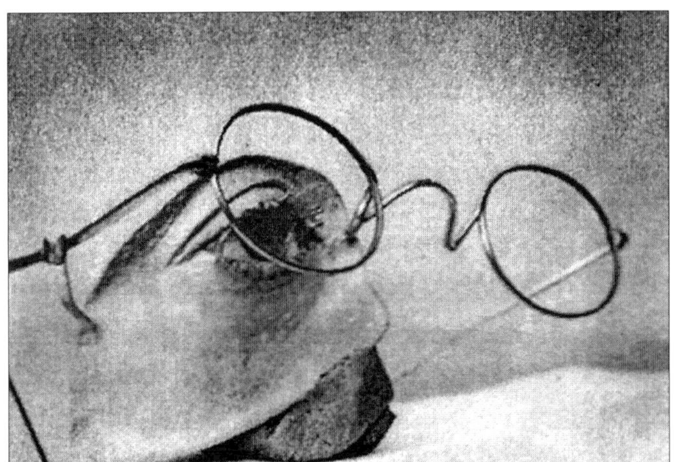

Fig 6 Eye mask with spectacles. Courtesy of the Lane Album, Anthony Wallace Collection, British Association of Plastic, Reconstructive and Aesthetic Surgery Archive. Reproduced with Permission.

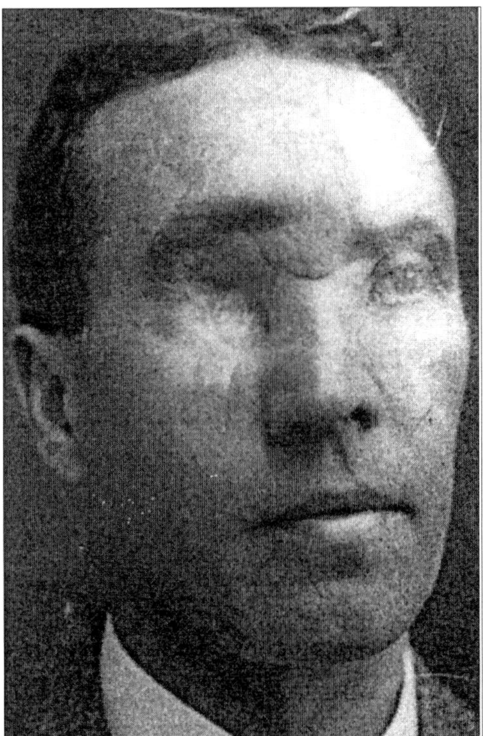

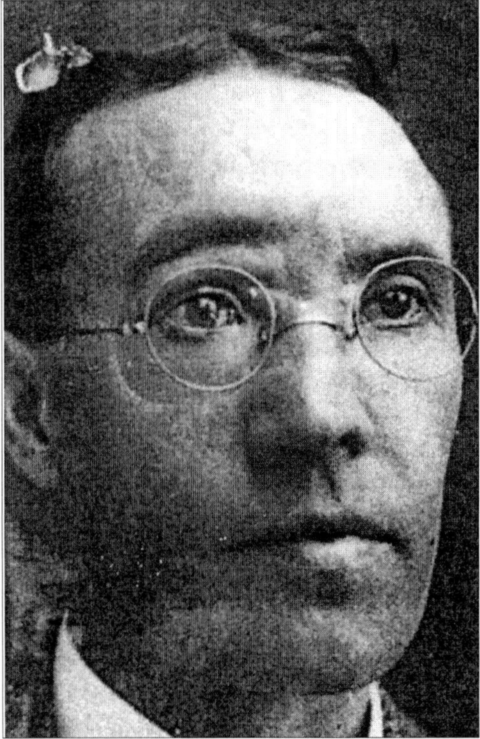

Fig 7 Man without mask. Courtesy of the Lane Album, Anthony Wallace Collection, British Association of Plastic, Reconstructive and Aesthetic Surgery Archive. Reproduced with permission.

Fig 8 Man with mask. Courtesy of the Lane Album, Anthony Wallace Collection, British Association of Plastic, Reconstructive and Aesthetic Surgery Archive. Reproduced with permission.

story of one patient who wore a mask home where it had the effect of making "his children flee in terror from the sight of his expressionless face" (Pound 1964: 35). These masks were an ingenious response to a terrible problem but they could not fill the vacuum of a missing face.

Custom Made and Standardized: The Significance of Prostheses

> I am made to model a chin for a man at the hospital. I feel terribly like God, the creator. The surgeon said with a smile, "Don't make it too long, or we shan't have enough to cover it." Sad! It's a fantastic world. (Scot 1949: 167)

The masks were just one of the many innovative and creative responses used by Sidcup to solve the problems posed by facial disfigurement. Sidcup employed a vast creative staff including sculptors, photographers and artists. These artists played a central part not only in recording the progress of the patients' recovery but also in the outcome of the patients' faces. Henry Tonks was a particularly notable figure in this field. Professor Tonks had been a surgeon before he became an artist. This background made him exceptionally useful at Sidcup because of his anatomical knowledge. His pastels and diagrams were not only vital in recording men's faces but also rebuilding them. Diagrams and sculpted models of the faces were used as the basis of the surgery (Figure 9). These methods were particularly important for the surgeons when the faces were so disfigured that there weren't any features to build on. One of the sculptors used by Sidcup in this period was Lady Kathleen Scot. Her influence over the outcome of the aesthetics of these rebuilt faces is powerfully expressed by her diary entry above.

The detailed, personalized and creative response that was used to treat facial disfigurement stands in stark contrast with the response to other types of disfigurement, such as the loss of limbs. This loss was treated with a standard response: amputation and restoration through a standard prosthetic limb. This limb was not personally designed but instead was simply measured to fit (see Guyatt 2001). It is this contrast between custom-made masks and mass-produced limbs that makes it poignant to question why these injuries caused such different responses. It was practical to custom-make these masks because of the smaller run of production and the various types of injuries and the various faces to which they were fitted (Feo 2007: 22). But these reasons do not explain the care and thought put into creating the face or making the mask which go beyond fitting the injury or creating said part. The thought behind the construction of the new face can be seen in Wood's words:

> The essential of the treatment is the restoration of features; the features may have been originally ugly or beautiful. As they are in life I try to reproduce them beautiful or ugly; the one desideratum is to make them natural. (Wood 1917: 949)

The governing concern therefore was to restore the face. The disfigured face was rebuilt whereas the missing limb was substituted, replaced by a standard prosthesis. The limb was not sculpted to restore the leg that was missing but made to fill its place, to fill the place of all missing limbs. For prostheses, aesthetic value was

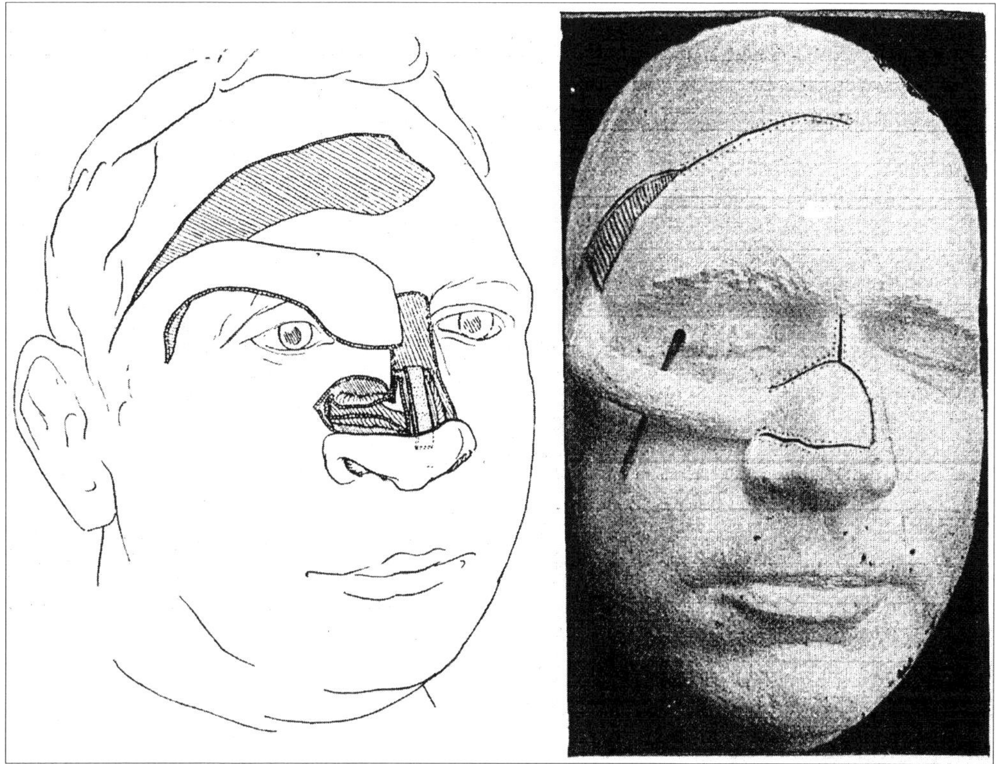

Fig 9 (left) Diagram of reconstruction and (right) cast of reconstruction. From Gillies (1920: 245).

a consideration but only after fulfilling the function of the limb. For those dealing with facial injury aesthetics was the central consideration, indeed for the masks the only consideration.

This difference in how the two injuries were approached highlights the importance of the face. The face had to be restored either as it had been, or to something passable as normal. The fact that the surgeons and artists slowly re-crafted a face rather than leaving it or substituting it outlines how vital an aspect of a person's humanity the face is. The worth in recreating the face and enduring the difficult process of facial reconstruction outlines its fundamental place in human interaction and social acceptance. Although other prostheses can be seen to have been used to indicate the soldiers' reintegration into society as they left the medical sphere (Gagen 2007: 533), the efforts to cure facial disfigurement departed from this platform as they were designed not only to cover the injury but to also to rebuild a man's identity.

Photographs Image and Identity

The photographs that fill Gillies' books and the Gillies archives are central to piecing together the history of the men who underwent these surgical procedures. The photos are significant not only in the subject matter they portray but also the function they play in the understanding the horror of war. The gravity of the shocking violence that is depicted acts to create a force that breaks momentarily the distance between the observer and the Great War (Callister 2007: 111). It is this force that caused Sandy Callister to cite Roland Barthes from *Camera Lucida*, "Contrary [to all other forms of representation, painting included] I can never deny that *the thing has been there*. There is superimposition here: of reality and of past" (Callister 2007: 112). The reality of loss, disfigurement, pain and horror are inescapable. This is outlined not only in the power of an image of unimaginable horror that replaces what once was a normal face but the intense focus of the image. The photos are close-ups, confrontational, fixed upon the sight of trauma, and as such one cannot escape the soldier behind the wound who was inevitably someone's husband, fiancé, brother or son. Humanity is instantly injected into the image. Unlike images of torn bodies and the dead amongst the mud of France, a face emerges that implies more than a number. Instantly upon viewing the face you wonder about their characteristics and lives, and you cannot deny the human suffering that has taken place. These photos are portraits of men of war; the depictions lock them in a moment in time, as part of a series of events that mark history in many different ways.

Compared to straight "portraits," however, the images lack the vital function of engaging with the sitter and their identity (West 2004: 29), although they are detailed studies of trauma and represent what has happened via destroyed and damaged facial features, they do not suggest any further characterizations. The photos were taken originally for a medical function, to catalog progress and to form the base of Gillies' teaching. Whether or not they were intended as portraits is not important, however; we read them via portraiture as the association of the face indicates the significance of our personality and character. Our face is inextricably linked to identity, how we recognize and identify with others, if we trust others, and how we prove our identity as in the case of a passport photo. The idea that identity is rooted in the physical self, the face (West 2004: 29), implies that the loss, or disfigurement, of the face therefore equates to a loss of identity. It is this circumstance of losing a face which, for Callister (2007:124), suggests a "primal terror" as the face is "a representation of our humanness." The loss of identity and humanity through this brutal disfigurement truly signifies why these injuries were so horrific for those who endured them and those who observed them.

The power of the photos in Gillies' textbook can be seen in the use of twenty-four similar images, from Jaques Joseph's clinics for the facially disfigured in Germany, in the postwar iconography of European pacifism in Ernst Frederich's Weimar pacifist text *War Against War* (1924). "No more horrible result of war," exclaims Sander Gilman (1998: 159), "could be represented in the public sphere than the mutilation of the face." Casts of these ravaged faces were exhibited in hospitals in France, Germany and King's Hospital London, where thousand of people visited on holidays in awe of the terrific suffering (Gilman 1998: 160). Yet images of these brutalized faces did not filter further into the public domain, which suggests that they may not have been acceptable for public consumption, or indeed nationalist agendas. Images of Sidcup that were in the public eye were of the officials and Royals on their visits,[1] the famous toy-making workshops or heavily bandaged soldiers. The official view of these injuries was therefore "public images of healing and rehabilitation rather then distress and trauma" (Callister 2007: 126).

Conclusion

The recreated faces discussed in this article highlight the specific importance of the human face, how it is central to communication, our ideas of identity and humanity. It is this that influenced both the treatment of injury and the reaction to it. Restoring faces through the creative programs of surgery and masks was an attempt to restore the young soldiers' identities as men. This was more than simply a matter of personal identity—it was about recreating a man's place in society and his humanity—and as such was significant on many levels, socially, personally, psychologically and professionally.

The unique power of the face in this case gives the photographs a special ability to describe the real horror of the Great War. It allows us to peel back the narrative and sterilized official history to see clearly the unimaginable human cost. This power is perhaps best described by C. S. Evans'

article in *Recalled to Life*, a journal that was published by the Ministry of Pensions for and about disabled soldiers. Evans describes the public queuing up to look at an ambulance train, at first he was sickened by the thought but then Evans remembered his own fascination at the beginning of the War with pictures of the conflict. He muses that this interest: "was not merely a morbid curiosity, neither theirs no mine, but rather a subconscious desire to realise a terrible thing concretely" (Evans 1917: 134). This is something that the tales and images of the facially disfigured do so well, transgressing the realities of horror that we understand but cannot comprehend.

The photographs that surround this topic are essential for describing the procedures, yet they also act to represent the unrepresentable in our imagination. Recreating this humanity was to "re-integrate a highly visible body back into its invisible normalised state"—to return to its place of one of many (Martin 2007: 317). It is this need to recreate these injured soldiers as whole, for them to be reinstated as "visibly acceptable," and to reintegrate them into society that pushed forward the innovative and creative responses of reconstructive surgery and facial masks during the Great War. Photographs were central to these responses and how we study them, pre-injury photos were used as main point of reference for recreating the face both for surgical and mask reconstructions. Photographs were used to document the amazing transformations, and for instruction. The photographs now form the basis of how we relate to the unimaginable trauma and mutilation and illustrate each stage of the procedure, thus fixing this subject in time and history and making it visible for future generations.

Note

1 For an example see Francis Lloyd signing visitors book in "*Rib to mend Jaw Bone*", how wounded soldiers are mended by new plastic surgery. *Daily Mail*, Friday July 27, 1917, p. 12.

References

Bamji, Andrew. 1996. Facial Surgery: The Patient's Experience. In Hugh Cecil and Peter Liddle (eds), *Facing Armageddon: The First World War Experienced*. London: Pen and Sword Paperbacks.

Bamji, Andrew. 2006. Sir Harold Gillies: Surgical Pioneer. *Trauma* 8: 143–56.

Barthes, Roland. 1981. *Camera Lucida. Reflections on Photography*, trans. R. Howard. New York: Hill & Wang.

Black, Catherine. 1939. *King's Nurse, Beggar's Nurse*. London: Hurst & Blackett.

Callister, Sandy. 2007. "Broken Gargoyles": The Photographic Representation of Severely Wounded New Zealand Soldiers. *Social History of Medicine* 20(1): 111–30.

Evans, C. S. 1917. On Convoy. In: Lord Charnwood (ed.) *Recalled to Life*, no. 1, June.

Feo, Katherine. 2007. Invisibility: Memory, Masks and Masculinities in the Great War, *Journal of Design History* 20(1): 17–27.

Gagen, Wendy. 2007. Remastering the Body, Renegotiating Gender: Physical Disability and Masculinity during the First World War. The Case of J. B. Middlebrook. *European Review of History* 14(4): 525–41.

Gillies, Harold and Millard, D. Ralph. 1957. *The Principles and Art of Plastic Surgery*. London: Butterworth.

Gillies, Harold. 1920. *Plastic Surgery of the Face; Based on Selected Cases of War Injuries*. London: Hodder & Stoughton.

Gilman, Sander L. 1998, *Creating Beauty to Cure the Soul: Race and Psychology in the Shaping of Aesthetic Surgery*. London: Duke Press.

Guyatt, Mary. 2001. Better Legs: Artificial Limbs for British Veterans of the First World War. *Journal of Design History* 14(4): 307–25.

Haiken, Elizabeth. 1997. *Venus Envy: A History of Cosmetic Surgery*. Baltimore: The John Hopkins University Press.

Lancet. 1916. Surgery. *The Lancet* 188(4870): 1109–10.

Lancet. 1917. The Queen's Hospital, Frognal, Sidcup. *The Lancet* 190(4914): 687–90.

Martin, David L. 2007. Of Monuments and Masks: Historiography in the Time of Curiosity's Ruin. *Postcolonial Studies* 10(3): 311–20.

Muir, Ward. 1918. *The Happy Hospital*. London: Simpkin, Marshall, Hamilton, Kent.

Pound, Reginald. 1964. *Gillies Surgeon Extraordinary*. London: Michael Joseph.

Scot, Lady Kathleen. 1949. *Self-Portrait of An Artist*. London: John Murray.

West, Shearer. 2004. *Portraiture*. Oxford: Oxford History of Art.

Wood, F. D. 1917. Masks for Facial Wounds, *The Lancet* 189(4895): 949–51.

**Photography
& Culture**

Volume 2—Issue 2
July 2009
pp. 195–200
DOI:

10.2752/175145109X12456654102885

Francis Bacon Archive, Tate Britain, London

Kathy Kubicki

Kathy Kubicki is Senior Lecturer in Photography, University College for the Creative Arts, Farnham, Surrey.

> I think of life as meaningless, but we give it meaning during our existence.
>
> Bacon, July 1973, interview with David Sylvester

The archive center at Tate Britain holds many treasures private and public correspondence, interviews and photos of past British artists and others.

Francis Bacon is probably one of the best known and most notorious of the British artists of the last century. His image, as seen generally via black-and-white photos, is by and large represented as angst-ridden poses, intense stare, wrinkled brow. Banished from his Roman Catholic Irish upper-middle-class family because of his homosexuality, Bacon was a self-taught artist, using art as a vehicle for his anxieties and as an expression of his level of belief in the power of art to change the way we see the world.

If we perceive Bacon as intense and worried it comes through these photos and many of the recorded interviews from TV and Radio also held at the Tate Archive Centre. We think of Bacon as an isolated soul, apart from his "drinking pals" in famous Soho watering houses such as the Colony Room. One interesting item discovered in the Bacon holding is a faded *Shell Road Map of Central London* from the 1970s. Bacon has drawn a line along his route from Rees Muse Studio to the famous Colony Room in Dean Street (now closed) where he spent a lot of time, not only a physical map, a mental map also, a safe route to wind his way home after one of his famous drinking sessions, where he often generously paid for everyone's drink throughout.

Bacon was hugely successful during his life time, he had a property in France and New York, but preferred his small London studio residence, two rooms in South Kensington, reminding us of how we are creatures of habit, and compounding the notion of "home" as something beyond the bricks and mortar of the place where we reside, where the local networks becomes crucial. Bacon befriended his neighbor Barry Joule, who did odd jobs for him and helped him out during his latter days. On the day Bacon flew off to Spain for his last retrospective he left a large case of source material and photos in Joule's charge. Joule took this responsibility seriously. Sadly Bacon never returned from his trip as he died in Spain the day before the show opened in Madrid on April 29, 1992. Joule did not open the case for some time but when he did he found a treasure trove of source material. Since that time he has donated this case and its contents to the Tate Archive in Milbank, London, and many other important institutions, such as the Pompidou Center in France, have benefitted from Joule's generosity.

The photos in this archive section are chosen for their ordinariness above anything else. Snapshots in faded 1980s film, they portray a side of Bacon we rarely see in the media and in all of the material that accompanies his blockbuster shows at major institutions. Here Bacon seems smaller than we imagine him, pensive, tentative, neither posing nor spouting rhetoric in the way that we are used to seeing him. In fact he was particularly and immensely articulate at talking about art, the grandness of that thing, the special position of the artist in society. Bacon's work uses found imagery as never before or since, perhaps Richter comes close,

but Richter's choices seem more ordered and practical. Bacon had an eye for detail, had a scopophillic drive to see through all the bad in society, and understood the power of media imagery, and the lie of mankind that says "love thy neighbor as thyself." He was particularly fascinated with death and torture, the Nazi Party and the horrific images of the concentration camps that circulated following the end of the Second World War, revolutions and wrestling. Bacon's range of imagery naturally chosen by him from magazines and books mirrors ideas in *Mythologies* by Roland Barthes (translated by Annette Lavers, Hill and Wang, New York, 1984) that everything is a text, in culture all things matter, are equivalent, worth examining.

In the photos here we get a feeling of *the everyday* of Bacon's life. Perhaps this is exactly the purpose of an archive. As Walter Benjamin states, we feverishly look for signs of the real in the paraphernalia of an archive, letters, receipts, and in the most powerful tool for this search, the photograph, the *imago*. In this selection of portraits of Bacon, we can imagine him as a real person, different but the same as us, as the process of identification takes place.

Bacon's intensity is laid to one side in these photos; maybe later in life he took comfort on a daily basis in his favored environment of South Kensington, as he had lost many close loved ones, sometimes in violent endings. Friendship and routine can override loss and bring refuge. Kinship and ritual is something we are all still attached to and drawn towards according to Freud. These are photos of days out and meetings with friends, intimate conversations.

Standing outside Seaton Place, Bacon is smartly dressed in a suit; he blends into the exterior gates in this photo, the faded pink and purple hue of this photo almost accidentally a commentary on Bacon's homosexuality. Yet we think also of the photographer and the relationship between photographer and sitter. In this case the memory comes from Joule, and to have spent time with this extraordinarily famous man and artist and yet have him merely and at the same time as the "man next door" feels like a privilege, an unexpected bonus for Joule, it changed his life in an everyday sense, and has had a profound affect for Bacon scholars and audiences since, just as these photos change the way we understand a part of Bacon's life usually ignored by the media, however in this case the myth of the artist's life as special is one that endures.

> I wish I wasn't so old. I feel there's such an infinite amount, which I shall never, never … I am far too old to ever be able to do it. I've got an infinite number of things I long to do … At the end of my life when I am dead, if anybody is in the least bit interested in my life, it (the work) will sum up what I thought. (Interview with Francis Bacon by Richard Cork for BBC Radio 3, *A Man Without Illusions*, May 1985)

Acknowledgements

With special thanks to the photographer Barry Joule, and to Adrian Glew at the Tate Archive, Hyman Kreitman Research Centre, Tate Britain, London.

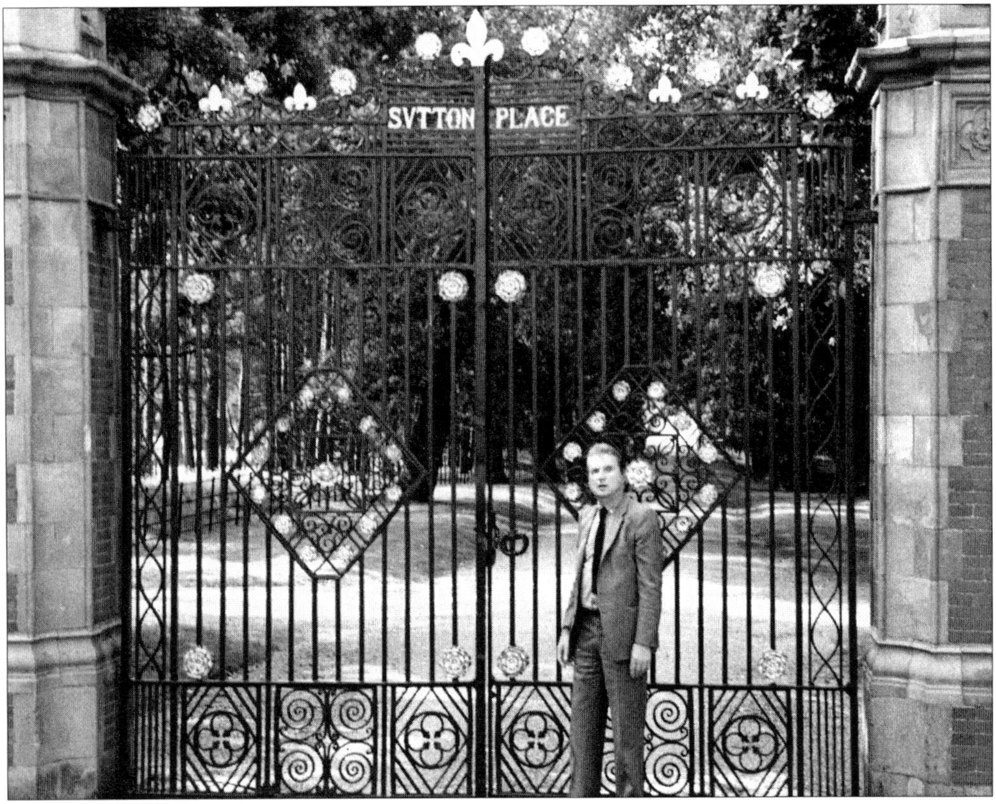

Fig 1 Francis Bacon standing outside Sutton Place. Courtesy of Tate Britain.

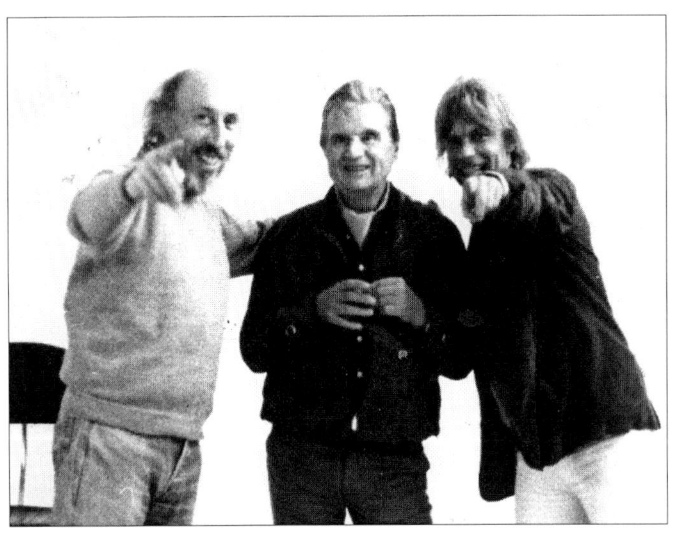

Fig 2 Richard Hamilton, Francis Bacon and Barry Joule (right) photographed June 1982, inside Hamilton's studio at North End Farm, Henley-on-Thames, where they spent the weekend. Courtesy of Tate Britain.

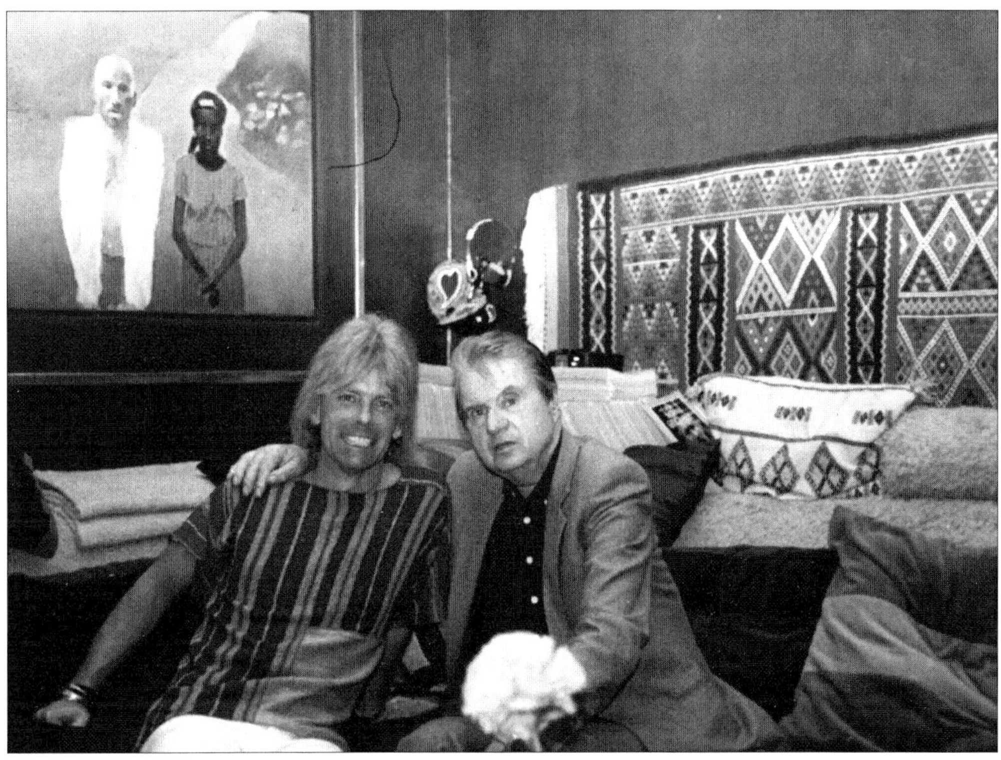

Fig 3 Francis Bacon and Barry Joule sitting together at no 5 Manson Place SW7 (Joule's flat 50 feet from Bacon's at 7 Reece Mews), July 1978, 1 month after Barry Joule first met Francis Bacon. Courtesy of Tate Britain.

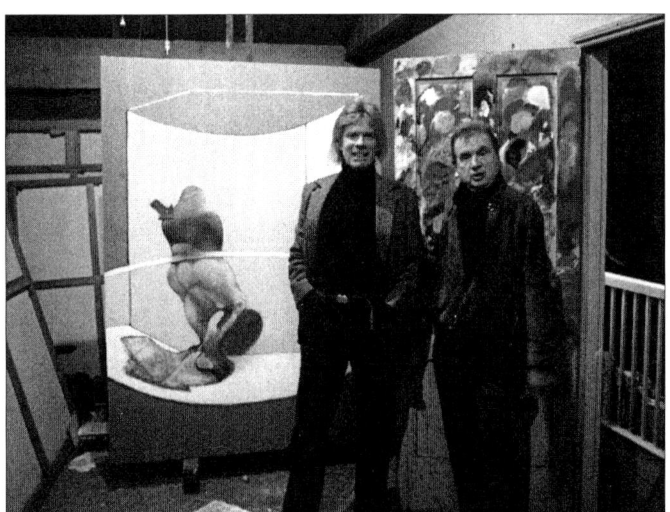

Fig 4 Francis Bacon and Barry Joule in studio at 7 Reece Mews, in front of just finished, not yet officially titled, but which they nicknamed "Big Yeller" and always called it that. Rudolf Nureyev the dancer came within a whisker of buying it hot off the easel. Photo taken March 1986. Courtesy of Tate Britain.

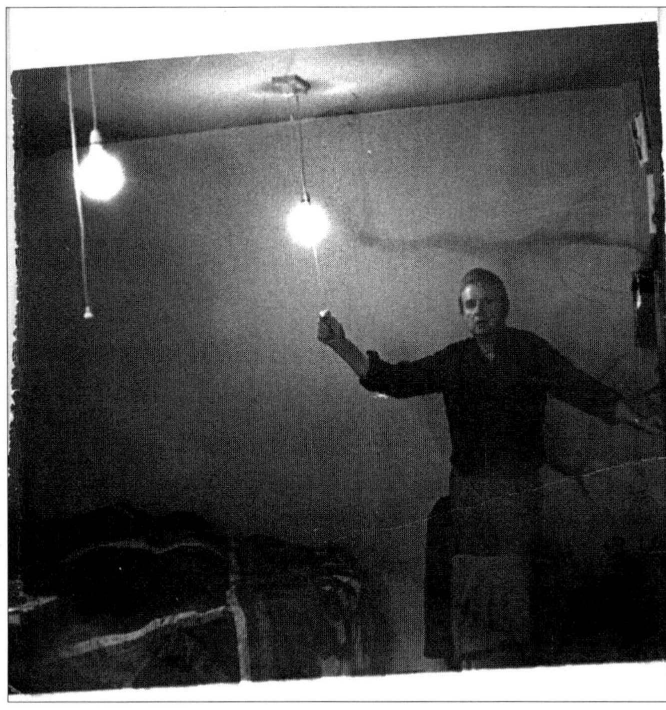

Fig 5 Francis Bacon turning on the light, June 15, 1982, at 7 Reece Mews. Courtesy of Tate Britain.

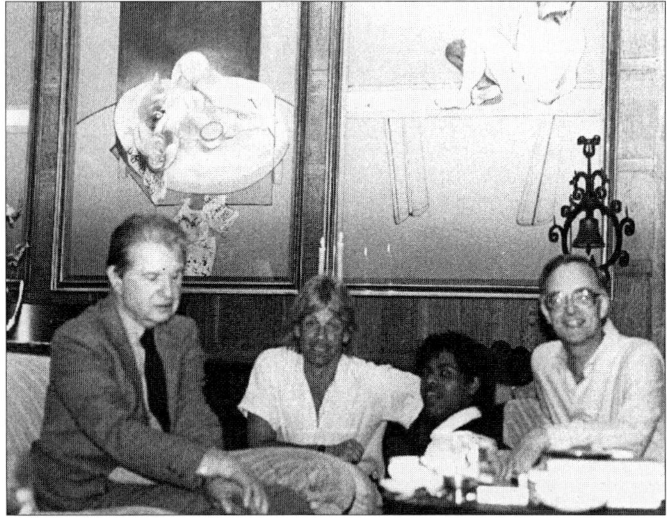

Fig 6 Francis Bacon, Barry Joule, Jay Rubillini and Roger Chubb (Director of Sutton Place) at Sutton Place, where they spent a weekend in May 1982 to see installation of newly purchased Francis Bacon "Triptych-Studies of the human body 1979," by the highly reclusive Stanley Seeger (American) the then owner of Sutton Place. Courtesy of Tate Britain.

**Photography
& Culture**

Volume 2—Issue 2
July 2009
pp. 201–204
DOI:
10.2752/175145109X12456654102920

Reprints available directly
from the publishers

Photocopying permitted by
licence only

© Berg 2009

Exhibition Review

Variable Capital

The Bluecoat, Liverpool, May 23–June 29, 2008
Curated by David Campbell and Mark Durden
Artists: Edward Burtynsky, Common Culture, Alexander
Gerdel, Richard Hughes, Melanie Jackson, Louise Lawler, Hans
Op de Beeck, Wang Qingsong, Julian Rosefeldt, Santiago
Sierra, Larry Sultan, Brian Ulrich, Andy Warhol

Reviewed by Chris Clarke

Chris Clarke is Curator of Education and Collections at the
Lewis Glucksman Gallery, University College Cork, Ireland.

Art and money. If the overriding attitude of modern artists
towards commerce was one of indifference or antagonism,
dismissed either as a crass devaluation of a higher, spiritual
pursuit or as a distraction from the integration of aesthetics
into politics, then contemporary artists have found the matter
more problematic. This exhibition, a fitting inauguration
to the Bluecoat's £12.5 million refit, might take its name
from Marx's definition of the wages paid for the production
of a commodity (the purchase of labor power), yet the
approaches on show reflect uncertainty towards the market
and frustration at the lack of alternatives. There's not much in
the way of utopianism here.

Take, for example, Brian Ulrich's photographs of retail
storage rooms, their shelves bursting with overstocked
and remaindered items. In *Untitled Thrift, 2006 [Britney]*, a
discarded Britney Spears display seems a cruel indicator
of obsolescence, of reification made real. The pop singer's
sleekly seductive and impenetrable image has quite literally
faded and worn out, relegated from shop floor to backroom
(or from stadium headliner to tabloid fixture). If Ulrich's
point is essentially a moral one, that the market's relentless
appropriation and consumption of the new has no time
for longevity, it is one that is developed further in Richard
Hughes' *Afterburner*, a matt of scuffed and battered cardboard
on the gallery floor. However, the marks here are deliberate,
the pattern of a bootprint marked in pigment and blended
into the stripped corrugation of the material, while the

embers of a squashed and stubbed cigarette remain dimly and perpetually, illuminated. Hughes turns refuse into spectacle and, consequently, reveals art's capacity to transform any image into a commodity, even an apparently anti-capitalistic one (as could be said of Ulrich's photographs).

A cynical observer might say the same of Santiago Sierra. While ostensibly critiquing the inequities of a globalized economy, his works exploit that same system, paying marginalized members of society (illegal aliens, drug addicts, prostitutes) a standard wage to enact "his" performances. *A worker's arm passing through the ceiling of an art space from a dwelling* and *eight people paid to remain inside cardboard boxes* are, as their titles suggest, attempts to inject transparency into the mechanisms of the culture industry. At the same time, there is a clear formal resemblance to key minimalist and conceptual artworks; Donald Judd's serial box-like sculptures, Robert Morris' choreographed columns toppling over on stage, even Robert Gober's eerily realistic wax leg jutting from the wall is echoed in a video of a disembodied arm dangling from the ceiling. Sierra's indictment thus reaches backwards to incorporate even these artists. In a similar way, Louise Lawler's photograph *Board of Directors* provides an unsentimental view of the art industry's so-called "economic power."[1] A partial view of Jasper Johns' *White Flag* painting is accompanied by the ubiquitous title card (with lot number, collection, details of verification, and the clincher: "Estimate: on request") as it is prepared for auction. That this work would go for $7 million, a record for a work by a living artist, is underscored by the list of Christies's Board of Directors underneath

the image. There is an acknowledgment of their role in conferring the monetary and art-historical value of the work whereby the painting and the artist's name become merely formal elements. As in Lawler's *Condition of Sale*, where paintings by Johns, Robert Rauschenberg and Roy Lichtenstein feature only as adjuncts to labels and estimates, the artwork seems unnecessary, acting only as a site for the circulation and speculation of commercial worth. Their black-and-white documentation and severe cropping renders any kind of aesthetic judgment impossible.

Faced with such a definitive, and pessimistic, verdict on contemporary art's complicity in the market, the other artists on show withdraw from a head-on confrontation, preferring to explore the secondary, spectacular aspects of capitalism. Edward Burtynsky's photographs of Chinese recycling landfills appear squalid yet sublime as do Wang Qingsong's elaborately staged images of tenement houses and sweatshops. A series of Andy Warhol's *Screen Tests*, near-static close-ups of various acquaintances, artists and studio regulars, reveal the artist's fascination with surface, shallowness and inscrutability. The labyrinthine structure of an exercise machine is equipped with video monitors (in Common Culture's *Because You're Worth it!*), tracking the gleaming limbs of powder-coated bright steel in an exercise of narcissistic self-reflexivity. Melanie Jackson's animated film follows the trajectory of consumerism, from advertisement to sales department, from manual labor (under armed guard) to assembly, shipping and reception, as a continuous loop, through "Guatemala, Russia, South Africa, Tajikistan, China, India,

Germany…" Perhaps, though, these various stances reflect a more localized approach of "microscopic attempts"[2] to transform society. Jackson's installation includes several boxes of free booklets, neatly circumventing the processes of capitalism displayed in her film. The Venezuelan artist Alexander Gerdel presents video documentation of *Workshop 69*, in which the artist hired two technicians to run a workshop in a gallery, repairing electrical goods. There is an emphasis here on grassroots politics, instances of generosity, practical measures and collaboration.

On the other hand, it could be said that such works are reactions to capitalism's unqualified hegemony, where "one wonders if artist and audience, seduced by this shimmering world have not been deflected away from the investigation of crucial issues about society's structure."[3] Larry Sultan photographs the interiors of houses in California's San Fernando Valley, a suburb which produces 80 percent of America's adult films and where a cottage industry of renting middle-class homes as film sets has emerged. In images such as *Hamner Drive* and *Kitchen Floor, Reseda*, he prioritizes the domesticity of the locations over the actual scenes taking place; shots between takes, of a naked actress squat on a towel, or a group of technicians perched on various pieces of furniture. There is no suggestion of the sex industry as a shady "other" to California's mainstream film production. Instead, it is made mundane, routine, unremarkable; a perfect indication of capitalism's complete integration into everyday life. One is no longer even able to differentiate between fantasy and normality, between the respectable and the perverse. All values level out, become exchangeable, under the common sign of currency. In *Den, Santa Clarita*, an ornate chair occupies center stage, its garish upholstery matched by paisley cushions, an Afghan rug, the intricate curves of a nearby dresser, and glass doors leading out towards the patio. Barely visible to the left is the backside and feet of a naked, kneeling woman, clearly engaged in oral sex just off-camera. In the midst of these surroundings, she is only another formal element, a piece of furniture, a commodity like all the rest.

Notes

1 Hans Haacke's *Manet-PROJEKT '74* attempted to trace the provenance of Manet's painting *Bunch of Asparagus* (1880) in the collection of the Wallraf-Richartz Museum, Köln. Due to historical connections and affiliations with Germany's Nazi period, the director Horst Keller rejected his proposal with the statement that: "A museum knows nothing about economic power. It does indeed, however, know something about spiritual power."

2 "Just as I think it is illusory to aim at a step-by-step transformation of society, so I think that microscopic attempts, of the community and neighborhood committee type, the organization of day-nurseries in the faculty, and the like, play an absolutely critical role." Félix Guattari, *Molecular Revolution* (Penguin, 1984) as quoted in Nicolas Bourriaud, *Relational Aesthetics* (les presses du reel, 1998).

3 Peter Halley, "Nature and Culture." In *Arts Magazine,* September 1983, reprinted in Charles Harrison and Paul Wood, *Art in Theory 1900–2000* (ed.) (Blackwell, 2003).

**Photography
& Culture**

Volume 2—Issue 2
July 2009
pp. 205–210
DOI:
10.2752/175145109X12456654102966

Towards an Impossible Closure—*Susan Meiselas: In History*

Reviewed by Maria Antonella Pelizzari

The work of Susan Meiselas questions, with a rare sensibility, the essence of photography vis-à-vis experience. Beginning in the early 1970s, as she immersed herself in situations that ranged from the local and familiar to the remote and extraordinary, she investigated the importance of history making and the frailty of witnessing that process as a photographer. As she stated

> the price of collecting information or news is at the cost of living like a human being. On the other hand, the price of becoming involved is that you may not be seen as a reliable witness. Sometimes I think that a photograph is *instead* of a relationship, and yet a photograph *is* a relationship.[1]

The current exhibition at the International Center of Photography (ICP), *Susan Meiselas: In History*, presents, in an exceptional overview and ambitious design,[2] the layers of complexity originated from these ideas. Not only is this the first time that a significant number of Meiselas's projects are brought together into one place, but the way in which these projects are showcased is remarkably tuned to this photographer's spirit. "This is not a retrospective," says the exhibition's curator, Kristen Lubben, as she explains that one of her main goals is to reveal that Meiselas' photographic encounters are "the beginning of something else."[3]

Indeed, the nature of this work is different from the documentary tradition concurrently presented at ICP—Cornell Capa's and W. Eugene Smith's. Unlike those linear picture-essays, Meiselas' photography brings together a dense palimpsest of moving images, magazines, scrapbooks, banners, postcards, and even matchboxes, which have unfolded, in time and space, from her still pictures. But what are the subjects of these pictures; and what makes Meiselas' encounters with them different from those of traditional "concerned photographers"?

The exhibition identifies three major involvements with a diverse range of communities: that with female strippers, recorded in New England carnival tents between 1972 and 1975; that with people of Nicaragua, represented before, during and after the revolution (1978 to 2004); and that with Kurdish survivors, retraced by her camera and historical research between a major genocide, occurred in 1988, and our time. The book that accompanies the exhibition brings these three chapters into a much larger context and helps tremendously to grasp the nature of her work. I was intrigued to learn about Meiselas' first photographic experiments, taking portraits of her peers in a boarding house in Cambridge, during her student years; and later, her educational work—in the South as well as in New York—using photographs as a means to collect personal stories. From the start, these series reveal Meiselas' awareness and anxiety about being an outsider, her diverse strategies in creating a dialog with all these "others," and letting them represent themselves. The interview between Lubben and Meiselas weaves all her projects into a cohesive totality, while scholarly essays reflect on the numerous themes that expand from her early uses of the camera (the engagement with individual communities; the importance of resistance; the meaning of photographic archives). Significantly, the design of the book speaks to the exhibition as it presents the layers of this visual history beyond the monographic approach, and,

most important, treats the photographs like artifacts. This volume, like Meiselas' books *Kurdistan: in the Shadow of History* (1998, reprinted in 2008) and *Encounters with the Dani* (2003) conveys the tactile pleasure of photographs as objects that one can cherish, exchange, circulate, consume and physically transform.

A selection of prints from *Carnival Strippers* (Meiselas' first book, published in 1976, and reprinted in 2003) is installed at the far end of the galleries, in a space made to look like one of those temporary tents where the strippers performed their shows. Entering inside this room is a bit like trespassing and this impression provokes a whole set of emotions that are connected to Meiselas' photographic experience: curiosity, trust, collaboration, fascination, compassion, and friendship towards these women. This self-directed exploration reveals the particular nature of a documentary work that has no pretense of amelioration or redemption, but, rather, aims to collaborate with these "others." Unlike Dorothea Lange, who, in front of the anonymous "migrant mother" felt that "she seemed to know that my pictures might help her, and so she helped me,"[4] Meiselas is not here to "help." Her photographs are a possible way to engage with the women and let them speak as individuals with a name. In the exhibition, an audio track hovers above the most intimate group of this series; in the book, a text runs parallel to the photographs. These words are tough, and the pictures support them as gentler evidence.

The intricate dialog between photographer and subject and the necessity to bring the photograph back to the community, as a means for oral history and personal storytelling, unfolds in Meiselas' lengthy involvement with Nicaragua.

Large color prints selected from her book hang from the ceiling and form a tight sequence of fragments—the photographers' fierce impressions of a revolution in the making. If some of these images resound, in subject matter, with the photojournalism of Cornell Capa (see, for example, Cornell Capa's record of the burning of Evita Peron's portrait, compared with Meiselas' brutal image of the flames wrapping a national Guardsman and the official state portrait of Somoza), the way in which these war photographs tell a story is radically different because of the context that surrounds them.

Along the lines of Victor Burgin's critique of the "purely visual," calling forth the "specificity of the social acts which intend that image and its meanings,"[5] Meiselas installed, a few years after the publication of the Nicaragua book, a project titled *Mediations*. As the title suggested, the project consisted in a study of the multiple interpretations and narratives built around those photographs, looking at which ones had been selected by the press, which ones had sold in the art world, which ones had been discarded in the process of editing the book, and which ones had been transformed into icons. Mediations, presented in England in 1984 and proposed, as an excerpt, at ICP, is a fascinating study of the migration and social appropriation of documentary images, as well as of Meiselas' inquiry on how images provoke stories, and whom do those stories belong to.

These concerns, and the importance of repatriation of pictures to the Nicaragua community, explain two subsequent film projects, *Pictures from a Revolution* (1991)

and *Reframing History* (2004), which surround the photographic installation. In the first film, Meiselas traveled back to Nicaragua with a small crew—her partner and film-maker, Richard P. Rogers, and Alfred Guzzetti—using her published book as a series of indexical traces of the people she had photographed. That particular copy of the book is in the exhibition case, as a visual clue to this important return trip, and a proof that it is possible to scribble a new story onto the surface of an old photograph. The book looks like a notepad, with names, phone numbers, addresses marked onto the white margins of the printed images. If *Pictures from a Revolution* reveals the photographer's self-questioning about the meaning of her work vis-à-vis Nicaragua's politics, the recent *Reframing History* attests to the transformation of photography into a memorial, a fragile monument indeed but a powerful and incisive one. In both cases, Meiselas acts as the invisible trigger for a history that belongs to these people. As she wrote elsewhere, "in doing this work, questions of authorship seemed secondary. I understood my pictures were a part of the Nicaragua's people history, and their history was more important than my pictures."[6]

The installation of the Kurdistan project appears the most successful in bringing together the seemingly contradictory threads of Meiselas' engagement with this community—that of being a photographer of their wounded territory and a collector of their historical pictures. Following her first exploration of deserted Kurdish villages in Northern Iraq (in April 1991), in December 1991 she was asked to join a forensic anthropologist, Dr. Clyde Snow, with Human Rights Watch, and document the aftermath of Saddam Hussein's "Anfal" campaign, occurred much earlier, in 1988. Many of those photographs are presented here for the first time (only a few were published in the Kurdistan book) and convey an overwhelming visual poem on human annihilation—images of ruins, concrete blocks that mark a mass grave, and, most striking, clothes unearthed in the attempt to identify those buried anonymously and left to signal the graves. These images whisper about the powerful and material affinity that exists between clothing and photography in relationship to death and disappearance— and they do so even more effectively than any Christian Boltanski's installation I have seen. This affinity is also powerfully conveyed through a series of photographs in which the Kurds are represented in the act of holding their personal images of the deceased and military fighters, showing their tremendous awareness about the value of those images as traces of their national identity.

But the meaning of these photographs goes much further. For one, they acted as proofs in the trial against Saddam Hussein, becoming decisive agents of history. To this effect, Meiselas' photograph of one of the very few survivors from the genocide, recorded with a bullet wound on his back, is presented beside a video of the trial in which that body belongs to a living person who is emotionally testifying against his killer. Here is a powerful example of a photographer's necessity to witness—without knowing that something so effective could come out of it.

The shift from this photography as agent of change to Meiselas' patient collecting of Kurdish visual history is extraordinary but difficult to comprehend for most people. Something happened to this photographer

as she stood in front of that evidence, feeling rather impotent and ignorant about the life of those people before the massacre. She visited their schools, saw photographs on their walls, and started to feel a new and possible relationship between herself and those foreign subjects through the depth of archives scattered throughout the world— from these people's backyards, to institutions in Paris and New York. As she explained, "we think of the field and the archive as so separate, but from me they ignite a similar response. The archive is a similar kind of retreat, where I can feel connected to community, where what I am doing makes sense."[7]

It does make sense to connect this operation to the earlier ones she performed in Nicaragua and in New England—there, also, her own photography was only partial in telling a story and another kind of narrative was sought after through those communities' involvement with her work. But the shift in Kurdistan is even more radical and it is no surprise that Meiselas' colleagues, picture-editors, and curators criticized her for not being the news photographer they liked to publish and exhibit. It is curious that this book brought me in close dialog with Meiselas for the first time as I became fascinated with her capacity to interrogate images, and wanted to know how a photographer had been able to achieve this.

The design of the show finds an interesting way to visualize the shift in Meiselas' work, presenting a digital projection that summarizes—with images and quotes— her basic interrogations at the time when she embarked on the archival research. The Kurdistan book—now reprinted with additional translations in Sorani (a Kurdish dialect) and in Turkish and presented in a selection of nine glass cases, each thematically different—discloses a full range of photographs, from chronicle to intimacy, that aim towards an impossible historical closure. Quite poetically, this volume suggests that one ought to try to piece together what seems irretrievably lost and that photographs are the essence of such a maddening jigsaw puzzle. Call it endurance, obsession, resistance or simply hard work. The way the layers of Kurdish history are presented in the form of passport photographs, postcards, album pages, travelers' records and published media is a celebration of the delicate, mysterious, hidden, and striking vulnerability of silver prints. One of Meiselas' thick spiral bindings shows the laborious process of bringing all these fragments into a book project, editing, revising, adding constant new information as it was coming in. Further down are records of Meiselas' return to northern Iraq, where amusement parks, oil refineries and shopping centers testify of a new regime and increasing historical complexities.

But if history goes on and this photographer continues to explore new formats for her visual explorations of marginal lives (a digital portfolio, titled "Costly Dream," where she has recorded domestic workers in Indonesia trained to go to Singapore—http://inmotion.magnumphotos.

com/essay/costlydream), the show offers a unique opportunity to stop and reflect on such unique engagement with the medium. This type of documentary approach promises resolutions through self-questioning, humility and even invisibility by essentially peeling away the skin of photographs, dismantling their authority and listening to their narratives with a great deal of passion.

Notes

1 These words are part of Meiselas' reflections on her work in Nicaragua, from the experimental documentary *Voyages,* produced with director Marc Karlin in UK in 1985. See the transcription of this project in Kristen Lubben (ed.), *Susan Meiselas: In History,* ICP & Steidl, 2008, p. 231.

2 The designer of this show is Dutch, Jeroen De Vries, who has worked with Meiselas on several projects in the past.

3 Lubben's words during an exhibition tour on November 21, 2008.

4 Dorothea Lange. 1980. The assignment I'll never forget. In Beaumont Newhall, (ed.), *Photography: Essays and Images.* New York: MOMA, 1980, p. 264.

5 Victor Burgin. 1982. Looking at Photographs. In *Thinking Photography*, London: Macmillan, p. 144.

6 Susan Meiselas. 1989. Some Thoughts on Appropriation and the Use of Documentary Photographs. *Exposure* 27(1): 14.

7 *Susan Meiselas: In History*, 2008, p. 243.

Photography & Culture

Volume 2—Issue 2
July 2009
pp. 211–216
DOI:
10.2752/175145109X12456654103000

Book Review

Motherland

By Simon Roberts, with an introduction by Rosamund Bartlett

London: Chris Boot Ltd, 2007. 192 pp.

Reviewed by George Slade

To create the photographs for his book *Motherland*, Brighton (UK)-based photographer Simon Roberts and his wife spent twelve months visiting sixty-five Russian cities, traveling 75,000 kilometers (45,000 miles) from coast to coast between August 2004 and July 2005. Besides the work, Roberts made a mark for himself in the chronicle of ambitious road trips. According to his notes and the very useful journey map on pp. 10 and 11, the trip began in Magadan, a littoral village in Far-East Russia, that has only one primitive road leading out, making air or water travel the normal modes of transportation. *Motherland* may not be an exhaustive account of a contemporary society but it's certainly exhausting to imagine. One supposes that the quest for thoroughness must have driven Roberts, even when automotive means failed to connect the city dots.

Would the old Soviet Union have allowed such a portrayal of its everyday face? How much of what Simon Roberts shows us in this book could he have witnessed in the more totalitarian, restrictive USSR of a generation ago? There's ample *glasnost* in *Motherland*, though to what end? And is it mutual? That is, is the photographer as open to Russia as the Russians are to him? The book delivers two visual pitches. One is a three-quarter or full-length portrait, not unlike those of Eve Arnold or Joel Sternfeld, in which an individual resides, graphically speaking, in a space that must serve as context, full of signs and symbols that impact our reading of the person as an agent of meaning. The second, contrasting with the portrait, is a medium-to-long shot that essays man's presence in, and culture's influence on,

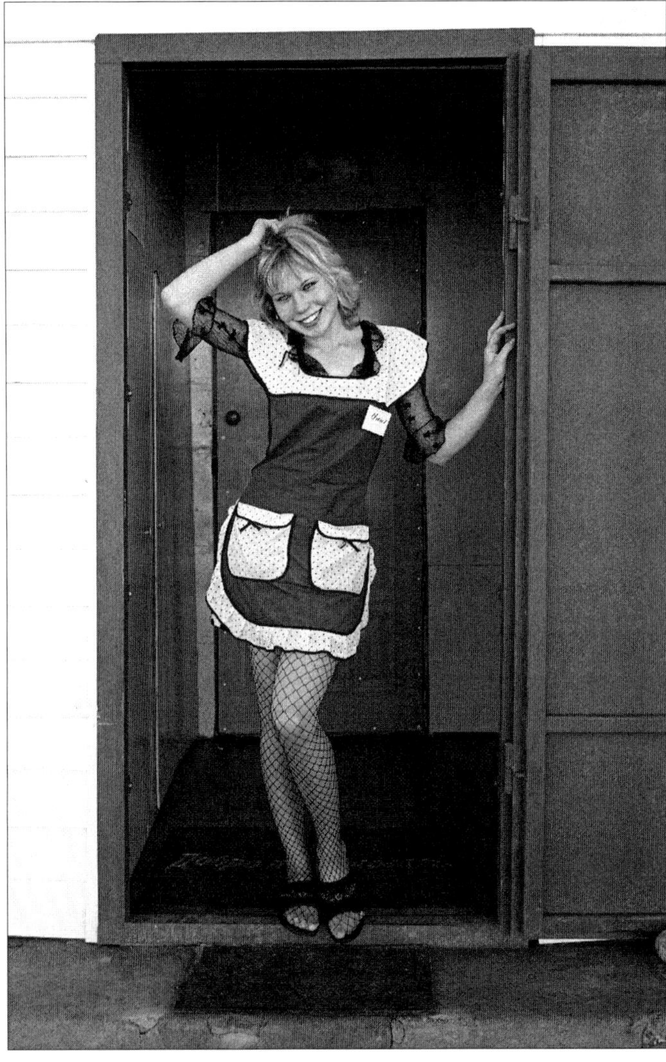

Fig 1 Evgenia Kuzminya, Magadan. Far East, August 2004. Evgenia Kuzminya is a student who works part time as a waitress at Café Pilot. She grew up on the Kamchatka peninsula but recently moved to Magadan to study dentistry at the university. The city's remote location means its cost of living is among the highest in Russia, and increasing economic difficulties and declining federal subsidies have led to a steady decline in the city's population. Photograph © Simon Roberts/ Chris Boot Ltd.

the natural landscape, though without the complications of an overt engagement with the players. Garry Winogrand used to say that a competent photojournalist needed to make only two kinds of pictures—the handshake, and the thoughtful shot of a guy alone on a beach. Something of that construct haunts this book, though the photographs sidestep such a reductive reading.

The "motherland" of Roberts's title is an approximate translation of the word *rodina*. It is a nationalistic loyalty that lies deep in the hearts of Russians. As Rosamund Bartlett

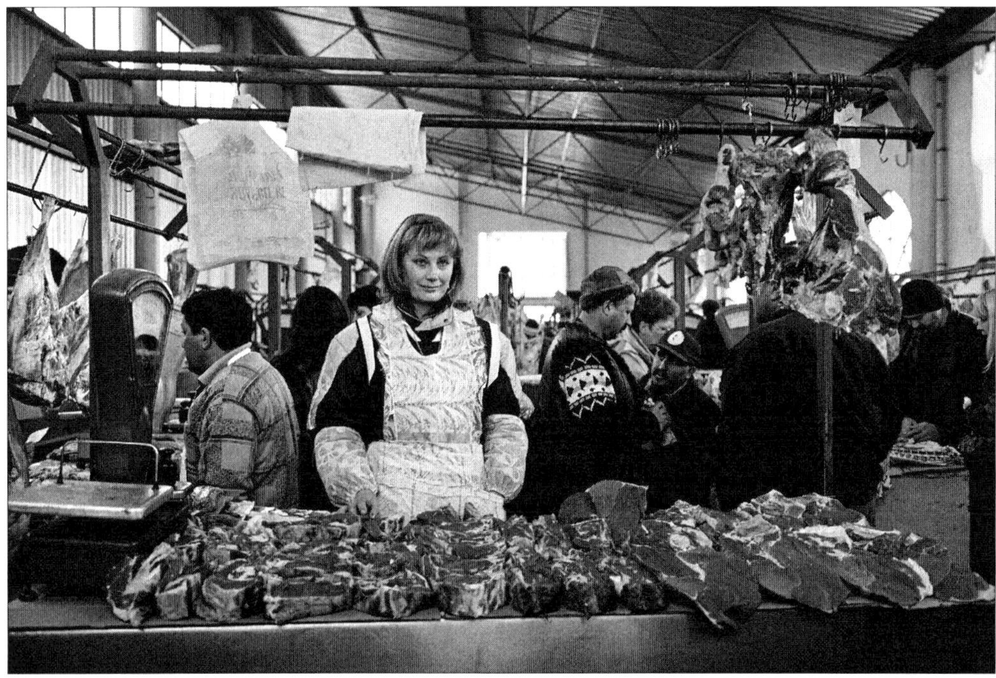

Fig 2 Meat market, Pyatigorsk. Northern Caucasus, March 2005. The city of Pyatigorsk sits at the foot of Mount Mashuk. The city was made famous by Mikhail Lermontov who, in an echo of the plot from his novel A Hero of Our Time, was killed here in a duel in 1841. Photograph © Simon Roberts/Chris Boot Ltd.

writes in her introduction, "The deepest source of patriotism in Russia … lies not in pride in national achievements or military glory, but in love for the motherland, whose most visible expression is the extraordinary, almost physical attachment which Russians have for their native landscape—an attachment which they are often at a loss to fathom." By identifying this chimerical, subjective phenomenon as the focal point of his study, Roberts has set a very high bar for himself and for photography. It seems that he has done a fine job of identifying the x and y axes; there are the people and there

is the landscape. It's the "almost physical" connecting tissue that's lacking, a third dimensional z axis that may be beyond the reach of anyone's camera. Nominally, there is no Zhivago-glorious, Tchaikovsky-lyrical, or even awe-inspiring Communist Russia in this collection, save for a handful of incidental Lenin statues. Roberts records diffidence and banality across the entire spectrum of twenty-first century Russia; if we are to discern *rodina* in these faces and spaces, it is a spirit exhausted from bearing the burden of empire for too many decades.

What is successful in the endeavor, though, is the true breadth of character apparent here under the nominal label of "Russia." There are many, many unexpected faces in the survey, and something terrifically appealing issues from such figures as rumpled, sun struck Vladimir, a harbor master in Kamchatka (p. 57), a vivacious waitress in Magadan (p. 21) and a lovely couple from Omsk portrayed in the front seat of their car, en route to their dacha (p. 147). Russia is the largest country in the world, covering about one-eighth of the earth's surface and perhaps one of the least densely populated (its 142 million people puts it ninth on the population top ten). Roberts deserves credit for having dedicated himself to charting and sharing Russia's many aspects; as the national entity charged since 1991 with maintaining the political role of the Soviet Union, Russia has carried on in a melting pot tradition almost as inclusive as that, historically, of the United States.

But questions intrude. Is it uncool to comment on cultural diversity in the twenty-first century? Is the aridity of much contemporary photography an artist's attempt to put emotional distance between the act of documentation and the attractions (admittedly challenging to depict) that drew one's interests in the first place? Roberts writes that "Russia has always fascinated me," and claims that "Spending a year there allowed for a sustained engagement with its landscapes and people." However, the scale of the subject and the enormous variety of its elements create a contradictory struggle between knowledge and thoroughness. That attraction evident in certain pictures, noted above, may have been an opening to the fuller, impassioned portrayal of *rodina*, a suggestion that Roberts, given his quest, may not have been able to explore, that photographs might evoke, or at least imperfectly translate, this sociologically specific quality. On the other hand, if the goal

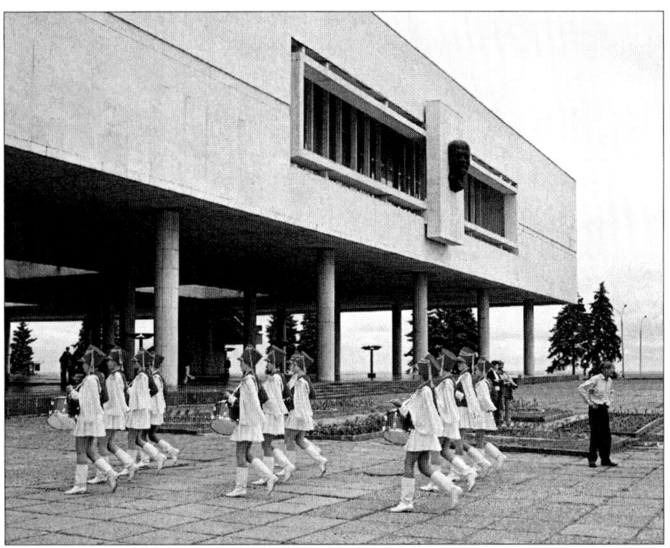

Fig 3 School band, Lenin Memorial Museum. Ulyanovsk Volga, June 2005. Vladimir Ilyich Lenin was born in the town of Simbirsk on 22nd April 1870. The town was later renamed Ulyanovsk in his honour, after his family name Ulyanov. Here a school band marches past the Lenin Memorial Museum, built around the original wooden house where Lenin was born and raised. Photograph © Simon Roberts/Chris Boot Ltd.

was a putatively "objective" study, a Sander (or Becher, or Gursky)-esque enumeration, Roberts might well have chosen a less nuanced target than what he refers to as the "nebulous spirituality" of *rodina*. Coquetteish Evgenia Kuzminya, working her way through dental school at Magadan's Café Pilot, is too three-dimensional to settle into a census.

Roberts's encounters with the broad phenomenon of contemporary Russia brush off the lingering implications of deeper knowledge or familiarity with place—the German typologists, while dry, still know their turf—in favor of quick confirmations of an itinerant nature, illustrations for an ethno-geographic taxonomy.

**Photography
& Culture**

Volume 2—Issue 2
July 2009
pp. 217–222
DOI:
10.2752/175145109X12456654103046

Book Review

Henri Van Lier: Philosophy of Photography

Barbara Baert, Jan Baetens and Hilde van Gelder (eds), with a foreword by Jan Baetens and Geert Goiris.

Leuven: Leuven University Press (Lieven Gevaert Series Vol. 6). 2007. 128pp. US$34.50.

Reviewed by Ulrike Matzer, translation: Richard Watts

Ulrike Matzer is a freelance art and cultural scientist based in Vienna and writes regular contributions on the theory and history of photography. Most recently she taught at the Academy of Fine Arts, Vienna (Department Art and Photography). She is currently working on her doctoral thesis on the subject of professional women photographers in the nineteenth century.

Philosophical questions arise whenever explanatory models from the various sciences are inadequate. In that light, the photograph—the first technical image to be used in a wide range of disciplines and forms, thus marking an epistemological watershed—would be a predestined subject for philosophy. It is all the more surprising that it disregarded this new medium for such a long time.[1] It was Vilém Flusser who first attempted to grasp photographic images in terms of the history of society from an explicitly philosophical viewpoint. His German-language essay *Für eine Philosophie der Fotografie* (in English, *Towards a Philosophy of Photography*) published in 1983 has meanwhile been translated into twenty languages. It is a classic of philosophical photography criticism, in which he subjects the machine-created image to an analysis in the context of an information society and closes with an appeal to the human critique of judgment.

A less well-known fact is that there was at that time already a French study with a similar title: *Philosophie de la photographie* by Henri Van Lier. For a long time it circulated more-or-less underground, which was due, in no small part, to its editorial history. The Belgium-based anthropologist and semiologist had conceived a series of lectures on the topic in Belgium in 1981, publishing them in 1983 in the *Cahiers de la Photographie*, whose editors Claude Nori and Gilles Mora published them ten years later as a book. However, the publishers soon went into insolvency. In 2005, *Les Impressions Nouvelles* wrapped the copies they had taken over in a fresh dust jacket to publish them as new at low cost.[2] The English translation of the essay, a quarter of a century after it was originally written, will now hopefully attract a wider audience. And offer a reading that takes into account the time of its writing.

Van Lier's study is quite a bit more extensive than Flusser's essay and he elaborates it essentially on the basis of the texture and structure of the photographic image, its genesis as a cut in space and time. Because of its physicality, he says, the photograph is capable of capturing the quantum nature of the universe. During exposure, photons strike halide crystals (or not) as a result of the wave-particle dualism of light, its constant speed and the discontinuity of its energy. Or, as Walter Benjamin metaphorically summed up this magic moment of exact technology: "for the tiny spark of contingency … with which reality has (so to speak) seared the subject."[3] From the latent image thus created

to the development of the negative and exposure on paper, he maintains, chemically induced energy transfers are involved, that, aleatorically and successively, necessitate multiple granularities, including the grain of the print, which many people generally associate with photography. Photography, he says, thus marries cosmology and technology. Van Lier explains these specific characteristics of photography, the imprint using light, with great precision.[4] A photon that can penetrate the lens and modifies the halides of the photosensitive layer is not a substance in the proper sense. It does transport energy, but not mass. So what is the status of a photographic imprint? Is it an index, as defined by the American semiotician and logician Charles S. Peirce,[5] a sign that is, by physical necessity, connected point by point with its object? In view of the randomness with which photons induce the darkening of the halides, and in view of all its abstractive qualities, it is not so easy to pin down the photographic process. Apart from the fact that it is only some short passages within his œuvre where Peirce theorizes the photographic image at all, he does not consider optical distortions, unevenly color-sensitive emulsions, chemical disruptions and the manual retouching of the pictures. Moreover, for him photography is also seen as an icon/simile and a symbol. According to Van Lier, these signs do not include photographs, because, unlike symbols (for example the words of a language), they are not founded on conventions. He also claims that an iconic similarity relation, as it applies to painting and drawing, does not apply to photography in this form.

To Van Lier, photon imprints are instead indices that refer physically to their cause.

"They are (very direct) indices of the imbuing photons, and, through their multiple abstractive mediation, they are (very indirect) indices of external objects and actions" (p. 36). In contrast, an index, in the sense of a deictic gesture, intentionally emphasizes the type of photographic image or parts thereof. This can be done by means of the choice of camera, film and filters, frame, lighting and the *mise en scène* of a motif, the possibilities of manipulation during development and printing, by means of subsequent retouching or, most clearly, by means of an arrow in the picture. Van Lier thus describes photographs as "contingently indexed indicial imprints." This may initially be confusing, considering that recent photo-theory discourses following Rosalind Krauss[6] commonly refer to a photo as an index, in keeping with the "index according to Peirce." Leaving Krauss unmentioned, Van Lier distances himself from Peirce, seeking instead to clarify linguistic concepts. For while English has only the word "index," French distinguishes between "index" and "indice." A "morphological accident"[7] that is caused by the pluralization of Latin words ending in -ex and that turns one *index* into several *indices*, thus resulting in some misunderstanding at least in photographic theory. Van Lier's distinction of the two terms, transferred into the English translation in the form of neologisms, brings into play a differentiation between what is objectively given and what is subjectively intended, the better to understand the contingent spatial-temporal interaction of photons, the photographic apparatus, the intentions of the person behind it, and what happens to the film after exposure as a process. This also manifests the dubious nature of Barthes's oft-cited referent: "Indices 'bring' or 'bear',

from the Latin verb *ferre*, but do precisely not re-fer, they carry but do not point, they signal but do not designate" (p. 121). The topoi of the *ça a été* [the *having-been-there*] and *le voici* are consequently deconstructed just as vaguely. For neither the thing nor its present perfect could be located precisely, and instead of "things" it would be more apposite to talk about instances-states. "Here," Van Lier says, is above all the photograph *per se*, in its materiality, and it is only by way of indexical rhetorics that it makes a reference to what it depicts.

Van Lier's definition, addressing the material aspect more strongly than the formal aspect in comparison with Peirce, proves to be practicable precisely in that respect. For by addressing its materiality, he focuses on the modes of use and effect of photography, its Protean nature, its "transmutability." Which makes reading his work rather useful when dealing with interdisciplinary questions, and not for nothing did Cultural Studies rediscover Van Lier.[8] For example, there are illuminating passages on commercial photography and other mundane images and on the characteristics of the slide, that is, in some cases, the only adequate means of visualizing reproductions created for art historical purposes, for example the paintings of Rembrandt. The luminous flux of a projected slide, he says, embraces the viewer almost architecturally, in contrast to the almost physical thickness of a Polaroid that by being unique represents a self-developing, autarkic world. With regard to pictures printed in photo novels, Van Lier observes that, in terms of their nature and sequence, they create non-situational situations in which the reader moves close to everyday life, but always in carefully demarcated fantasies.

Despite illustrative examples such as this, the book is in parts difficult to understand. This is probably not only due to the fact that the author draws on the methods and knowledge of such diverse disciplines as mathematics and quantum physics, psychoanalysis, phenomenology and philosophy, semiotics and linguistics, the history of art and culture, anthropology or "anthropogeny," as he terms the science that he himself developed, and how he associates all of this. The fact that he uses common terms in an uncommon manner, as in the case of index, is also a little confusing. According to him, photon-darkened grains are *analogical*, whereas the contingency that decides whether a halide crystal is hit, as if between 0 and 1, is *digital* in the sense of calculable (even if, one might add, the process is as a whole amorphous and incalculable from the outside). This is just one point among many that would certainly be worthy of considering and developing. For, as mentioned above, the text was written in 1981, one year after *La chambre claire* [*Camera Lucida*] and at the threshold of the increasing use of digital technologies in photography. It is hard to say whether a broader reception of Henri Van Lier's philosophy would have caused the discourses of "post-photography" to take a different turn to Roland Barthes's authenticity-invoking ontology of the photographic image. Where Barthes's book may be read as a kind of autobiographical novel, sprung from his yearning imagination, Van Lier treats various photographic behaviors, of which Barthes's Oedipal behavior is one of many, on a theoretical, critical level. It is certainly

worthwhile reading Van Lier and Barthes in parallel, as is viewing him in context with Flusser's essay, in which the latter not only understands and treats the "apparatus" in a similarly extended sense, but also describes the structure of the photographic gesture as an explicitly quantum one: "a doubt made up of points of hesitation and points of decision-making."[9] Reading Van Lier's work may also be helpful in drawing up a more accurate definition of current hybrid forms of analog and digital technologies, something that, with regard to the book's illustrations, students of the Hogeschool Sint Lukas, Brussels, apparently already put into practice. By philosophically questioning seemingly fundamental certainties, seeing the specific characteristics of the photography medium as intrinsically differentiated, as hybrid, Henri Van Lier's book possesses many topical aspects that reach far beyond the time of its writing.

Notes

1 Cf. The survey of Michaud, Y. 1994. Formes du regard. Philosophie et photographie, in M. Frizot (ed.), *Nouvelle Histoire de la Photographie*. Paris: Bordas, pp. 730–8.

2 Which would also increase the visibility of Van Lier's second essay devoted specifically to photography: Van Lier, H. 1992. *Histoire photographique de la photographie*, Paris: *Les Cahiers de la Photographie*. An English version can be found on the author's website: http://www.anthropogeny.com.

3 Benjamin, W. 1931. Little History of Photography, trans. E. Jephcott and K. Shorter. In W. Benjamin. 1999, *Selected Writings*, M. Bullock and M. W. Jennings (eds), vol. 2, part 2, 1931–1934. Cambridge, MA: Belknap, p. 510.

4 A fact that Philippe Dubois also confirms. Cf. Dubois, P. 1983. *L'acte photographique*. Bruxelles:

Labor—a book whose main ideas to some extent go back to Van Lier.

5 Alongside Ferdinand de Saussure, founder and American representative of modern-day semiotics (1839–1914). An appendix to "Peirce and Photography" is found in the mentioned volume.

6 Cf. Krauss, R. 1977. Notes on the Index: Seventies Art in America (Part 1), *October* 3. Cambridge, MA: MIT Press. Krauss, R. 1977. Notes on the Index: Seventies Art in America (Part 2), *October* 4. Cambridge, MA: MIT Press, pp. 58–67. In her detailed and highly illuminative essay on the French reception of Rosalind Krauss's notion of the index around 1980, Katia Schneller traces the shift from a theoretical topic initially elaborated within the context of art history (as a critique of modernist medium specificity) to the domain of the history of photography, by delineating the French-American intellectual exchanges during those years. She also outlines the vivid Belgian semiotic field, with Henri Van Lier as a central character, and Philippe Dubois whose photography theory related him to Rosalind Krauss. Schneller, K., 2007. Sur les traces de Rosalind Krauss. La réception française de la notion d'index. 1977–1990. *Études photographiques* 21: 123–43.

7 Cf. Van Lier, H. 1981, *Logique de dix langues indo-européennes (Le français dans le monde). Complément 2: L'anglais et la mer*, www.henrivanlier.com/anthropogenie_locale/linguistique/compl2.pdf (accessed January 25, 2009).

8 Accordingly, Jan Baetens described photographs as "objects in action" during the colloquium *La photographie au regard des théories de la communication/Photography as Culture and Communication* that he co-organized for the book presentation, Leuven and Louvain-la-Neuve, May 30 to June 1, 2007. The aim of the colloquium was to find out in what manner of image-text relation Van Lier's (also) semiotic instruments could be used. Photographic archives, the city as text, photo novels, photographed writing were just some of the topics of the lectures. A volume of selected contributions to the conference will be published soon in the series of the Lieven Gevaert Research Centre for Photography.

9 Flusser, V., 2000. *Towards a Philosophy of Photography*. London: Reaktion Books, p. 39.

**Photography
& Culture**

Volume 2—Issue 2
July 2009
pp. 223–226
DOI:
10.2752/175145109X12456654103082

Book Review

Women's Albums and Photography in Victorian England: Ladies, Mothers and Flirts

Patrizia di Bello

Aldershot, Hampshire and Burlington, VT: Ashgate, 2007

Reviewed by Juliet Hacking

Juliet Hacking studied for her BA, MA and PhD at the Courtauld Institute of Art. From 1996 to 1999, she was a part-time visiting lecturer at, consecutively, the Universities of Derby and Reading and at the Courtauld Institute. In 1999 she joined the National Portrait Gallery where she curated the exhibition (and wrote the catalog) *Princes of Victorian Bohemia: Photographs by David Wilkie Wynfield* (Prestel/NPG, 2000). From 2000 to 2006, she was a specialist in the Photographs Department of Sotheby's auction house (Head of Department from 2003). Dr. Hacking is currently Programme Director of the MA in photography (contemporary and historical) at Sotheby's Institute of Art, London.

A number of photo-collages found in women's albums from the mid-nineteenth century are striking for their playful subversiveness. Having long been appreciated by curators, art historians and students as photomontage *avant la lettre*, references to these albums in historical texts have nonetheless served to identify them as meaningless rather than meaningful. In this book-length study, Patrizia di Bello sets out to challenge the idea that album-making was nothing more than the product of genteel female boredom and constriction. In order to do so, she situates women's albums in relation to the pre-photographic models that informed their assembly, to the dominant models of genteel femininity purveyed by publications aimed at women, and to the creative interventions made by the specific women who collated them. Di Bello is scholarly and rigorous in her approach, claiming historical specificity as necessary to test a scholar's assertions. And yet the book is not simply an "old school" research project. The author also wanted to see "what would happen" if these albums were subjected to "formal, social, semiological and psychoanalytical scrutiny" (p. 10).

In the first chapter, di Bello accounts for how photographic albums, and the "professional" photographic portraits they so frequently contain, were marginalized by a modernist Anglo-American history of photography as too commercial, too domestic and too feminine for the canon. Highlighting the clear iniquities of this assessment, such as the fact that Charles Lutwidge Dodgson carefully arranged his photographs in albums, di Bello argues that the (assembled) photographic album is, in the wet-collodion era, an object of considerable social and cultural significance. The albums she discusses were compiled by titled or well-connected middle-class women caught between two overlapping models of genteel femininity: the wife/mother of the domestic realm and the socially obligated wife. The drawing room, where photographic albums were perused both privately and socially, was where she was called upon to be both. Di Bello summarizes the album's role in the domestic culture of display: "The album publicises the interiority of the woman of the house by making it visible" (p. 41).

It is di Bello's contention that certain nineteenth-century albums speak of and to the pleasures and pressures of negotiating these competing roles. Informed in her approach by Jo Spence's practice and by feminist social histories and cultural theories, di Bello is not looking for these albums to tell us how things were, but about the aspirations, desires and anxieties that would have been engendered by culturally constructed ideas of the feminine. As a mass-produced visual media, photography is one means by which nineteenth-century women are offered "imaginary possessions":

> Albums, with their fragmented, collaged and compressed spatial organisation, were part of a female visual culture that women could use to articulate their experience of what, in modern society, they were offered only to be denied: success as a mother in the case of Anna Waterlow, success in aristocratic society, in the case of Lady Filmer. (p. 27)

Collecting photographs is, di Bello argues, one of a number of domestic pursuits that speaks of gentility when it is about exchange rather than purchase; when it is a display of inventiveness, discernment and skill rather than evidence of passive consumption. Her large aims are to see how her subject elucidates "wider aspects of the cultural experience of women in the nineteenth century" (p. 24) and to claim the photographic album as one of Griselda Pollock's "spaces of femininity" (p. 26). If di Bello cannot reclaim the albums for modernism, she believes it is possible to do so for modernity.

The complexities of class and status identification, so frequently overlooked in studies of nineteenth-century photography, are here brought to the fore. The competing roles for women who wished to be perceived as gentlewomen of taste were negotiated across a variety of sites: serious periodicals, popular journals, annuals and picture books, novels and advice manuals. One of the key points that di Bello makes is that these publications were all pre-photographic, as was the practice of album making. Her case study for the pre-photographic album is the one compiled in the early nineteenth century by Anna Birkbeck, daughter of a Liverpool merchant and married to George Birkbeck, the founder of Birkbeck College. As di Bello demonstrates, Birkbeck's album (comprising drawings, watercolors and inscriptions made on the page) speaks of activity not passivity, and is about the construction of a social milieu designed to be "read" by others. By the time that Anna Waterlow, married to Sydney Waterlow, the upwardly mobile head of a London printing works, compiled her *photographic* family album (c.1850–c.1870), albums such as Birkbeck's were considered out of date. And yet, for all her engagement with the modern medium of photography, Waterlow's album is, according to di Bello, as much about intimacy and proximity as Birkbeck's. Lady Filmer, married to Sir Edward Filmer, compiled her album in the 1860s before having children. Her photo-collages are here linked to her flirtation with Albert Edward, Prince of Wales; both, it is argued, are empowering, active, social games of intimacy and evasion.

We have grown somewhat unaccustomed to the significant point made with a light touch and so it is important to emphasize the contributions this book makes to the fields of nineteenth-century studies, women's studies and photography. Through her commitment to historical specificity, di

Bello not only reclaims these albums from the patriarchal assumptions of modernist art history, but also from universalizing cultural theory that refuses to test the idea by reference to the object. While the discussion of tactility (or the "haptic"), maternal desires and anxieties and feminine sexuality are not new to the subject of nineteenth-century photography, di Bello seeks to anchor them in the epoch that produced them rather than our own. Her subjects are not makers of photographs but the consumers. This shift from production to consumption reinforces two key points: that respectability was not entirely a matter of socio-economic demographics and that popular visual culture was hugely significant in the construction of models of feminine gentility. Throughout this text, agency is restored to "the angel of the house." Flirtation is reclaimed as an activity that would not necessarily result in social censure. And, when di Bello subjects the photographic family album to psychoanalytical scrutiny, something fascinating does indeed happen: we see the woman turning its pages as able to enjoy as well as mourn the erosion of her maternal role.

The one notable weakness of this otherwise excellent study may, ironically, be a by-product of di Bello's rigor. Her methodological approach demands that she brings to bear upon her chosen subject current scholarship in social, art and photographic history, critical and cultural theory and detailed empirical data. It also demands that her arguments are worked through a number of photographic albums compiled by genteel Victorian women—or so one would have thought. So much time is spent building the bigger picture that the author only discusses two albums in any detail (and not as much detail as she suggests). Although di Bello does invoke other "mixed media" albums, her remarks are cursory and the reader is referred to the texts in which they have been discussed by other scholars. It would have been more convincing if the author had tested her analysis against these other examples; in particular, the photo-collage album compiled by Princess Alexandra (Royal Collection, Windsor Castle) that she mentions in passing (p. 131) poses the important question as to whether middle-class album-makers were aping royalty or vice versa. Also, in seeking to implicate these albums in the notions of status, taste and femininity mediated by a variety of cultural forms, it seems an oversight not to discuss the relevance (or otherwise) to her study of other forms of cultural production, such as painting (other than Frith's *The Railway Station*) and drawing-room comedies (pre-Oscar Wilde).

On its own terms, the book succeeds in claiming femininity, photographic albums and photo-collage for modernity. But, I would argue, this is not its most important contribution to scholarship. It was (let's not forget) the privileging of modernity that engendered a patriarchal modernism, and left us with the Western cultural paradigm that claims only the encounter with the new, and radical ruptures with the past, to be of cultural relevance. While we might believe that we have deconstructed modernism's ideological bases to the point it cannot function in the present, modernism (with its firsts, its greats, its uniques) is alive and well as the language of commodity culture and the art market. Di Bello's study is all about reclaiming shifts in social and cultural life as "a matter of degrees and nuances" (p. 41); it foregrounds continuities and assimilation, and the interplay between identification and evasion. According to di Bello, these albums are significant because they celebrate relationships and aspirations not governed by the marketplace; according to this reviewer her book is significant because it celebrates scholarship on the same terms.

Photography & Culture

Volume 2—Issue 2
July 2009
p. 227
DOI:
10.2752/175145109X12456654103127

Reprints available directly
from the publishers

Photocopying permitted by
licence only

© Berg 2009

Books Received

Erika Barahona Ede. *Retratos*. Museu Valencia De La Il-Lustracio I De La Modernitat-Muvim, 2008.

Richard Benson. *The Printed Picture*. New York: The Museum of Modern Art, 2008.

Yvonne De Rosa and Laura Noble. *Crazy God*. Bologna: Damiani, 2007.

Regis Durand, Douglas Park and Alexander Garcia Duttman, *Commonsensual: The Works of Rut Blees Luxemburg*, London: Black Dog Publishing, 2009.

Michael Fried. *Why Photography Matters as Art as Never Before*. New Haven, CT: Yale University Press, 2008.

Louis Kaplan. *The Strange Case of William Mumler, Spirit Photographer*. Minneapolis: University of Minnesota Press, 2008.

Robin Kelsey and Blake Stimson, eds. *The Meaning of Photography*. Williamstown, MA: Clark Art Institute, 2008.

Karen Knorr. *Fables*. Paris: Filigranes Editions, 2008.

David Moore with text by Chris Petit and Angela Weight. *The Last Things*. Stockport: Dewi Lewis Publishing, 2008.

Abdi Roble and Doug Routledge. *The Somali Diaspora: A Journey Away*. Minneapolis: University of Minnesota Press, 2008.

Ana Teresa Ortega. Foto-Esculturas. Enric Mira, Alvaro de los Angeles, 2006.

Barbara Thompson, ed. *Black Womanhood: Images, Icons, and Ideologies of the African Body*. Seattle, WA: University of Washington Press, 2008.

Varvara Shavrova. *Untouched*. Timezone 8, 2008.

PHOTOGRAPHY & CULTURE
Notes for Contributors

Manuscript Submissions

The Editors welcome submissions that explore issues related to the areas described in the *Photography & Culture* journal description document. Indeed, any relevant aspect of *Photography & Culture* will be considered as long as *both* those elements form the core of the submission. It is requested that plain language be aspired to, with the use of jargon or specialized terminology kept to the absolute minimum. (Where specialized terms are unavoidable, please supply a glossary.) All submissions considered for publication will be subject to peer review.

Submissions aimed at being major articles should be approximately 3,000–10,000 words in length and *must* include a brief (two- or three-sentence) biography of the author(s), an abstract (up to about 200 words) and up to five keywords. Shorter papers ("Notes") should range between 500 and 2,500 words in length. Interviews should not exceed 15 pages (about 4,000 words) and do not require an author biography. Exhibition and book reviews are normally 500–2,000 words in length.

Electronic submissions (preferred, certainly in the first instance) should be sent to photographyandculture@ bergpublishers.com. Microsoft Word is the preferred word-processing program, where possible. Scanned illustrations will suffice, though originals may possibly be requested in certain circumstances if the submission is successful. (Originals will be returned.) Please scan to letter or A4 size at 300 dpi for photographs/halftone, or 600 dpi for maps or illustrations containing text. Illustrations embedded in Word documents cannot be used. Similarly, graphics downloaded from webpages are not of sufficient quality for print reproduction.

A disk as well as a hardcopy of any finally accepted contributions may occasionally be requested. (Please mark clearly on the disk what word-processing program has been used. Berg accepts most programs with the exception of Clarisworks.) Manuscripts or disks should be submitted to the current *Photography & Culture* postal address: Photography & Culture, PO Box 11, Moreton-in-Marsh GL56 0ZF, UK.

Submissions will be acknowledged by the managing editors, and those accepted for further consideration will be entered into the review process. Electronic manuscripts and scanned illustrations will not be returned. Submission to the journal will be taken to imply that the article is not being considered elsewhere for publication, and that if accepted for publication it will not be published elsewhere, in the same form, in any language, without the consent of the editors and publisher. It is a condition of acceptance by the editors of a submission for publication that the publishers, Berg, automatically acquire the copyright of the published article throughout the world. *Photography & Culture* does not pay authors for their submissions nor does it provide retyping, drawing, or mounting of illustrations.

Style

The journal's text will use US spelling and mechanicals. *The Chicago Manual of Style* (15th Edition) is our style guideline, and *Webster's Dictionary* is our arbiter of spelling. While it would be preferred if contributors used US English, submissions in British English will be acceptable (though such submissions will be transliterated into US spelling and mechanicals). We encourage the use of major subheadings and, where appropriate, second-level subheadings. Manuscripts (whether electronic or hardcopy) submitted for consideration as articles must contain: a title page with the full title of the article, the author name(s), address and affiliation where relevant (do not place the author name(s) on any other page of the manuscript), a two- or three-sentence biography for each author, and a 200-word abstract. Up to five keywords are requested to aid in any future library searches. Please present the keywords after the abstract.

Electronic manuscripts can be either single- or double-spaced. If hardcopy manuscripts are involved, then they must be typed double-spaced (including quotations, notes, and references cited), one side only, with at least one-inch margins on standard paper using a typeface no smaller than 12-point. Authors should retain a copy for their records.

It would be preferred that submissions be presented with paragraph breaks involving a line space (double line space if presenting a double-spaced text, of course) between paragraphs and without first-line indentation, as in this set of guidelines.

Notes and References

References to *notes* are to be by means of consecutive numbers inserted in-text throughout the paper and are to be written up at the end of the text. (Do not use any footnoting or end-noting programs that your software may offer as this text becomes irretrievably lost at the typesetting stage.)

For *references*, the "Harvard system" is to be used in-text, thus:

> Centuries ago in Europe, country people were terrified of the walking dead, of "revenants" (Smith 1989). They developed all kinds of protective procedures (Jones 1957; Morris 1972, 1984), and though these may seem bizarre to us now they were deemed absolutely necessary at the time.

The cited references should be presented at the end of the paper, after any notes, in this manner:

References

Dewdney, S. 1962. *Indian Rock Paintings of the Great Lakes*. Toronto: University of Toronto Press.

Dowson, T. 1992. *Rock Engravings of Southern Africa*. Johannesburg: Witwatersrand University Press.

Fagg, B. 1957. Rock Gongs and Slides. *Man* 57: 30–2.

Goldhahn, J. 2002. Roaring Rocks: An Audio-Visual Perspective on Hunter-Gatherer Engravings in Northern Sweden and Scandinavia. *Norwegian Archaeological Review* 35(1): 29–61.

Hedges, K. 1990. Petroglyphs in Menifee Valley. *Rock Art Papers* 7: 75–82.

Lawson, G., Scarre, C., Cross, I. and Hills, C. 1998. Mounds, Megaliths, Music and Mind: Some Thoughts on the Acoustical Properties and Purposes of Archaeological Spaces. *Archaeological Review from Cambridge* 15(1): 11–34.

Palmer, D. and Pettitt, P. 2001. In Search of our Musical Roots. *Focus* 105: 80–4.

Rajnovich, G. 1994. *Reading Rock Art: Interpreting the Indian Rock Paintings of the Canadian Shield*. Toronto: Natural Heritage/Natural History Inc.

Reznikoff, I. 1995. On the Sound Dimension of Prehistoric Painted Caves and Rocks, in E. Taratsi (ed.), *Musical Signification*. Berlin: Mouton de Gruyter.

Rowland, I. and Howe, T.N. (eds.) 1999. *Vitruvius: Ten Books on Architecture*. Cambridge: Cambridge University Press.

Offprints

On publication, first-named authors will be sent a PDF eprint (with nonprinting watermark) of the final, published version of their article for personal use, and will be able to order a free copy of the issue in which their article appears.

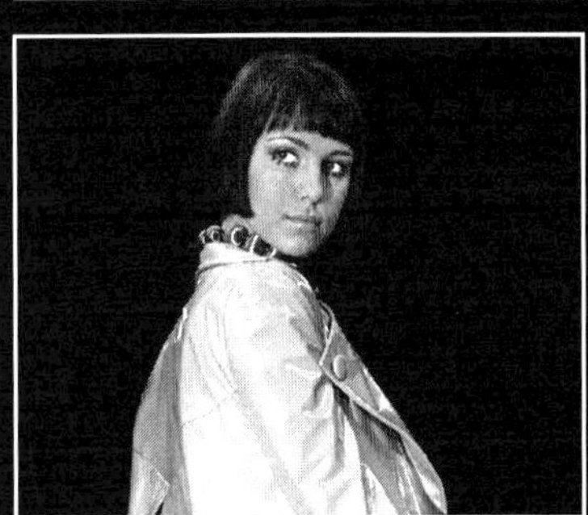
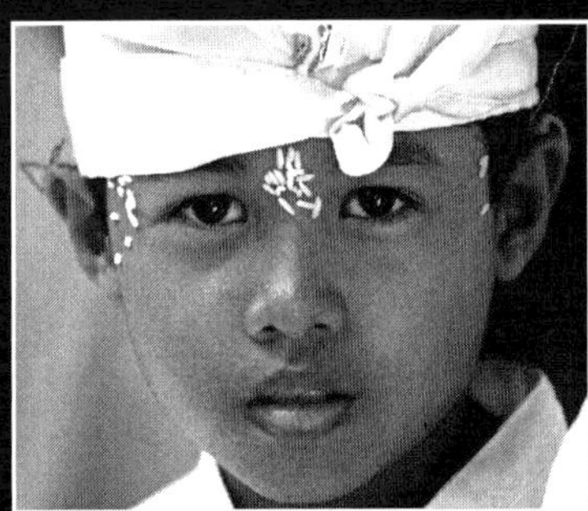
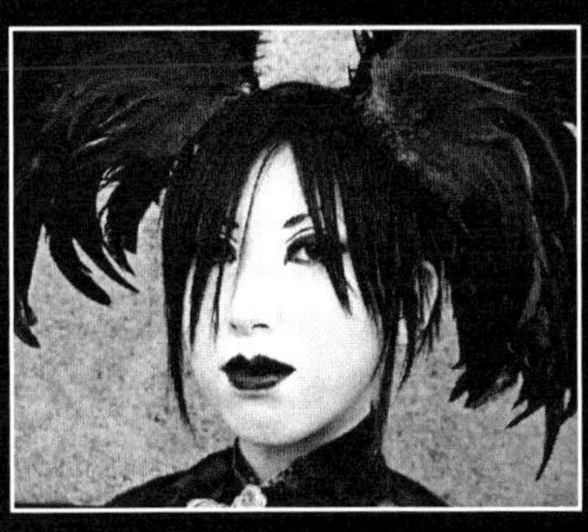

Visual Sense: A Cultural Reader

Edited by

Elizabeth Edwards and Kaushik Bhaumik

Vision is more than looking or seeing. It is integral to all human action. Visual Sense introduces students to the analysis of a wide range of ways of experiencing sight across time and across cultures: from Renaissance Italy, Aztec Mexico and early Christian Europe, to Tibet, West Africa, Aboriginal Australia and South America, amongst others. It is arranged around broad themes of visual experience, ranging from navigating the sacred and ordering knowledge about the world to thinking creatively, socially and beyond vision into cyberspace and daydream. This unique approach allows cross-cultural and thematic connections to be made. A Guide to Further Reading allows students to expand their learning independently, and section introductions place the readings in context.

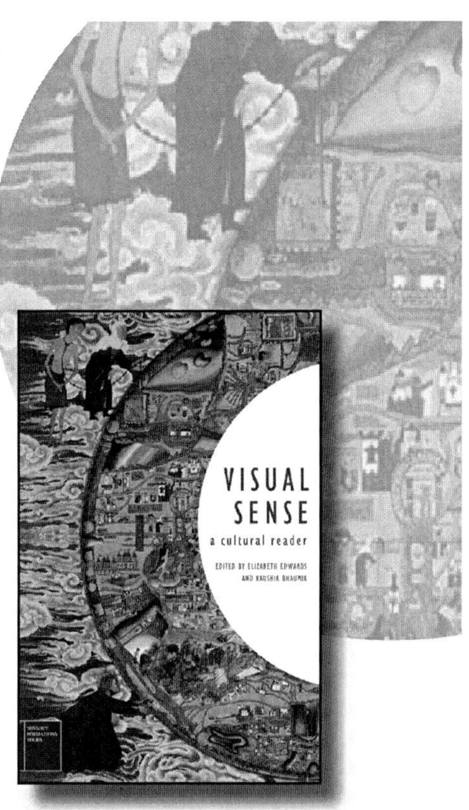

Nov 08 • 496 pp • 15 bw illus • 234 x 156 mm
HB 978 1 84520 740 3 **£60.00 / $119.95**
PB 978 1 84520 741 0 **£19.99 / $34.95**

Visual Impact
Culture and the Meaning of Images
Terence Wright

From the office to domestic interiors to shops, images surround us in modern life. Pictures and images provide a cognitive context through which people can explore and understand their world. The internet has increased this visual onslaught exponentially. Is there a systematic order to this seemingly endless array of pictures and depictions?

Drawing on a wide range of examples – from painting and drawing to film, photography and the Web – Visual Impact analyzes the theory and practice of visual representation, and examines how cultural values and traditions shape particular visual styles.

Visual Impact sets image making in an historical and global context, and uses it as a window for exploring the human condition at a deeper level. Anyone interested in the cultural role of art, film, the internet and interactive media will find this book an exciting and stimulating read.

Dec 08 • 192 pp
20 bw illus • 234 x 156 mm
PB 978 1 85973 473 5 **£19.99 / $39.95**
HB 978 1 85973 468 1 **£55.00 / $109.95**

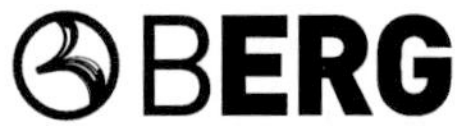

Order now at www.bergpublishers.com